CULTURES OF THE WORLD

BELGIUM

Robert Pateman

MARSHALL CAVENDISH
New York • London • Sydney

Reference edition published 1995 by
Marshall Cavendish Corporation
99 White Plains Road
P.O. Box 2001
Tarrytown
New York 10591

© Times Editions Pte Ltd 1995

Originated and designed by
Times Books International, an imprint of
Times Editions Pte Ltd

Printed in Singapore

Library of Congress Cataloging-in-Publication Data:
Pateman, Robert.
    Belgium / Robert Pateman.
      p. cm.—(Cultures Of The World)
    Includes bibliographical references and index.
    Summary: Introduces the geography, history, government,
economy, culture, and people of the small European country
of Belgium.
    ISBN 0-7614-0176-8 (lib. bdg.)
    1. Belgium—Juvenile literature. [1. Belgium] I. Title.
II. Series.
DH418.P38 1995
949.3—dc20   95–14900
               CIP
                AC

INTRODUCTION

The Kingdom of Belgium is one of Europe's smallest and most densely populated countries. It lies at an important crossroads of canals, rivers, and motorways, and a great deal of Europe's trade passes through the port of Antwerp. Belgium's location has not always been to its advantage; many times in its history, the country has been conquered or used as a battlefield by other nations.

Belgians speak two different languages: in Flanders in the north of Belgium, people speak Flemish (a version of Dutch), and French is spoken in southern Wallonia. A great deal of attention has been paid to the linguistic and cultural differences in Belgium, but at the same time there are many unifying influences—most of all, people's pride in the prosperity and achievements of their small nation.

CONTENTS

Although it is highly industrialized, Belgium is still dotted with farms. The ground surrounding stables and other farm buildings in Belgium is usually paved; otherwise, in the rainy season, the movement of farm animals makes the courtyard muddy.

CONTENTS

The Assumption of the Virgin, one of Peter Paul Rubens' masterpieces.

GEOGRAPHY

COVERING 11,781 square miles (30,513 square kilometers), Belgium is approximately the same size as Rhode Island and is slightly bigger than Maryland. Even at the widest point, it is only 180 miles (290 kilometers) across. On a map, Belgium's shape resembles a bunch of grapes.

Its important network of canals, rivers, and highways connects the country to eastern and western Europe. The Belgian coastline faces the United Kingdom and the North Sea, one of the world's busiest waterways. The north and northwest parts of the country are low-lying; gently rising plateaus and hilly forests dominate the southern and eastern regions.

Belgium shares borders with the Netherlands to the north, the Grand Duchy of Luxembourg to the southeast, Germany to the east, and France to the south and southwest.

Belgium's only natural boundaries are the 42-mile (68-kilometer) North Sea coastline in the northwest and the Meuse river, which for a short distance marks the border between Belgium and the Netherlands.

The Semois river gently winds through the Ardennes, then enters France, where it joins the Meuse river.

Opposite: **The forest landscape in southern Belgium, as seen from a hot-air balloon.**

7

FERTILE PLAINS AND UNDULATING PLATEAUS

Belgium can be divided into six main regions:

FLANDERS LOWLANDS On the coast of Flanders is a narrow belt of lowlands, reaching from the borders of France to the Schelde river. The area has many fine sandy beaches and dunes. Behind the dunes lie the *polders* ("POHL-duhrs"), land reclaimed from the sea and protected from floods by the natural barrier of dunes and artificial sea walls. The *polders* are formed by thin, sandy soil overlying clay and require heavy fertilization before they can be farmed.

Inland, the plains of Flanders extend southwest and are crossed by the Leie, Schelde, and Dender rivers. Intensive farming and industrial development characterize this area.

THE CENTRAL LOW PLATEAU rises to 700 feet (213 meters) in the south. It includes Belgium's best farmland, due to the region's rich alluvial soils.

The Senne, Demer, and Dijle rivers cross the plateau toward the Rupel river, ending in the Schelde river. Once covered with forests, the landscape has now been transformed by dense human habitation. Light industry is common along the region's impressive road network, but the typical vista is still that of farmland dotted with small villages. Brussels, the capital of Belgium, lies at the center of this region.

The sand dunes along the North Sea coast prevent the sea from flooding the lowlands during high tide.

BELGIUM

Feet   Meters

1640   500
660   200   Lowlands
0   0

0   30 Miles

0   30 Kilometers

Concerns about the environment have arisen in the last few years. One of the biggest issues is the condition of Belgium's beaches, where the sea is often considered unhealthy for swimming. In the summer, during the tourist season, samples of sea water are analyzed daily.

THE KEMPENLAND PLATEAU In the north, by the Dutch border and between the Schelde and Meuse rivers, rich farmland gives way to a region of sandhills, scrub moorland, and coniferous forest. Coal deposits in the region once provided almost all the coal Belgium needed.

The Kempenland is now a mining and industrial center. The region also has an atomic research and nuclear power center, a recycling plant, and a large army base. Passing through pleasant wooded countryside, the Albert Canal, which links the Meuse and Schelde rivers, carries barge traffic on the way to Antwerp. Newly built roads connect the region to Belgium's major cities and to Germany's industrialized Ruhr valley.

9

THE SAMBRE-MEUSE VALLEY This narrow but well-defined region is approximately 100 miles (161 kilometers) long but only 3 to 10 miles (5 to 16 kilometers) wide. Extending from the south to the north of Belgium along the Sambre and Meuse rivers, the valley connects the central low plateau to the higher plateau of the Ardennes region. Coal mining used to be the main industry here, and it supported other heavy industries; thus this region became one of the most populated in Belgium.

THE ARDENNES lies east of the Sambre-Meuse Valley. This was once a large mountain range, but the mountain tops were long ago worn down by glaciers. Today the Ardennes region consists largely of sandstone ridges, limestone valleys, and woodland hills rising above 1,000 feet (305

The area south of Namur city in the Sambre-Meuse Valley has many fascinating caves rich in stalactites and dramatic rock formations. Some of the caves have rivers flowing through them and have been opened to tourists.

RIVERS

Belgium's river and canal system has played an important role in shaping the country's economy.

The Meuse is a gently flowing river that starts in eastern France and runs north into Belgium. It has cut a steep, narrow valley through the Ardennes, and it flows past the city of Dinant before joining the Sambre at the city of Namur.

The Meuse continues to flow north, collecting other rivers as it goes. It flows into the Netherlands, and from there enters the sea south of Rotterdam. The Meuse is nearly 600 miles (965 kilometers) long, and ships can sail down much of this length. Where the river is too shallow to allow ships to pass, canals have been cut. Of all the navigable rivers in Europe, only the Rhine is more important.

The Schelde is 270 miles (434 kilometers) long and is a vital link in the European transportation network. The river starts in northern France and flows past Gent, where it is joined by the Leie river. It then takes a northeasterly direction, eventually reaching Antwerp, a major port. The building of new locks has enabled the harbor facilities to extend another eight miles (13 kilometers) down river. (A lock is a portion of a canal with gates at either end, the closing and opening of which adjusts the water level in that part of the canal.) About 20,000 ships dock in Antwerp every year: an average of 54 every day. From Antwerp it is still another 55 miles (88 kilometers) to the sea.

meters). Close to the German border are some high hills: the Botrange is the highest point at 2,277 feet (694 meters), and the Baraque Michel rises to 2,111 feet (643 meters). The Ardennes region has excellent hiking trails, fast-flowing rivers, and winter snow, making it a major recreational area.

BELGIAN LORRAINE, located at the extreme southeastern point of the country, rises to more than 1,300 feet (396 meters). Part of the Paris Basin, soils here are far more fertile than in the bordering Ardennes. Farming and agriculture are the main occupations. Some iron fields support steel mills and other industries, but this has not stopped the migration of its population to the cities.

CLIMATE

Belgium has a reasonably gentle maritime climate. Generally, summers are warm without becoming hot, winters cold but seldom severe. Winter temperatures usually vary between 37°F (3°C) and 52°F (11°C); summer temperatures are around 70°F (21°C). Although the weather is mild, there are long periods of dull, gray days with abundant rain. There is no striking difference in the climate from one part of the country to another, but there are some minor regional differences.

In the Ardennes, a typical year will bring anything between 140 to 150 days of snow. Because the area is not particularly high, the snow does not last very long.

The coastal areas particularly can have a day-to-day weather pattern that is different from the rest of Belgium. Often it is dry along the coast when it is raining in the rest of the country, and because of the warming influence of the sea, winters are generally milder. Oostende, at the Belgian coast, averages about 1,760 hours of sunshine each year, but Brussels, less than a hundred miles (161 kilometers) away, gets around 1,585 hours.

The hilly terrain of the Ardennes also creates its own weather pattern: more rain and cooler temperatures. Only the summer months, from May to early October, are free of frost. Usually the area has heavy winter snows.

For most of the year, the winds blow from the west from the vast expanse of the Atlantic Ocean. Winds occasionally come from the east, across the Eurasian land mass, bringing snow, storms, and periods of unusual cold in winter and heat waves in summer.

FLORA AND FAUNA

In the past, Belgium was covered with deciduous forests. Oak was the most common tree, but beech, birch, and elm also thrived. Over the years, much of the original forest has been cleared for farmland or housing. The country's wildlife has been greatly affected by the destruction of the forests, but the Ardennes is still a major refuge for animals such as boars, red deer, wildcats, and tree martens. The coastal region has its own rich fauna. This area is a vital resting ground for migrating birds and a winter home for many northern birds.

Belgium has several national parks and reserves. The Hautes Fagnes Nature Park, the largest of these, covers boggy fenland east of the Ardennes and extends over the border into Germany. Although the area is not as remote or wild as it once was, trekkers have to be careful there, particularly in bad weather. The Lesse and Lomme National Park is much smaller but protects a beautiful stretch of the Ardennes riverside. On the coast toward the Dutch border, the Zwin Nature Reserve covers a tidal wetland area that is an important reserve for over a hundred different species of birds as well as the unique dune vegetation. Farther south, the Westhoek Nature Reserve has been set up to protect 840 acres (340 hectares) of sand dunes. As building continues along the coast, this might soon be the last area to retain the coast's original appearance. Despite these efforts, much of Belgium's wildlife, including some of the bat species and many wild plants, are still endangered.

In summer, golden fields of wheat are often dotted with red poppies.

MANNEKEN-PIS

Manneken-Pis has become the semiofficial symbol of Brussels and is one of the most famous landmarks in Europe. Nobody really knows why the statue was built, but there are numerous tales of its origin.

One version suggests the statue is that of an unknown boy who, needing to urgently relieve himself, made the mistake of doing so outside a witch's house. The angry witch allegedly turned him into a statue. In another story, the statue was put up by grateful parents whose son was found on this spot after wandering off during a busy carnival. A more unlikely account is that the statue honors a little boy who saved the city by putting out a fire.

Manneken-Pis was originally a stone statue, carved by Jérôme Duquesnoy in 1619, but that earlier version was replaced by a bronze model in 1817. Since then *Manneken-Pis* has been stolen by several invading armies but has always found its way back to the city.

Manneken-Pis has over 500 costumes for special occasions. On September 3, he is dressed in the uniform of the Welsh Guards, the unit that liberated Brussels from the Germans in 1944.

Opposite: **According to a Flemish legend, a giant would chop off the hands of any sailor who did not pay a toll when sailing into the Antwerp harbor. The severed hands were thrown into the Schelde river. He was stopped by a Roman soldier, Silvius Brabo, who cut the giant's hands off. Brabo's statue now stands on Antwerp's main square, and some people say the name of the city, *Antwerpen*, might well come from this legend—a combination of the words *hand* (hand) and *werpen* (to throw).**

CITIES

BRUSSELS is the capital of Belgium and, including the suburbs, is home to about 990,000 people. The capital is at the hub of Belgium's road and rail networks, and the international airport is only nine miles (15 kilometers) out of town. The city has both tram and subway systems.

Brussels has been chosen as the headquarters of many international organizations, including NATO and the European Union. Its major industries include mechanical engineering, foods, textiles, chemicals, and printing; construction work is also very important. In recent years, modern electronics factories have opened in the suburbs.

ANTWERP is Belgium's second largest city and is home to nearly half a million people. It is the fifth busiest port in the world and, after Rotterdam in the Netherlands, the second busiest in Europe. In addition to being an important industrial city, Antwerp is also a major diamond center: 40% of the world's cutting and 70% of the polishing trade are conducted here.

GENT, also known as Ghent, was a Roman city that grew into a great trading center during the medieval period. Magnificent buildings of that time still stand, including the town hall, cathedral, and cloth hall. Much of Gent's charm and character comes from the many branches of the Schelde and Leie rivers that flow through the town. Gent is also a thriving modern city, with a steelworks and factories that produce paper, chemicals, cars, and electrical goods. Although it is over 20 miles (32 kilometers) from the sea, Gent is linked to the coast by a canal and has an important harbor.

LIÈGE has been a regional capital since the Middle Ages. It stands where the Meuse meets the Ourthe river and is Belgium's third largest city. Liège was the site of the first coal mine in Belgium and developed early as a commercial, financial, and industrial center. Various wars and battles over the years have destroyed much of the old city.

BRUGGE, or Bruges, is sometimes called the Venice of the North because of its canals, bridges, monuments, and buildings—some of them dating from the 15th and 16th centuries. The city was once one of the greatest commercial cities in Europe. Today it is a major tourist town, but there are also breweries and other industries. Brugge is linked by a canal with the port of Zeebrugge about seven miles (11 kilometers) to the west.

HISTORY

WE KNOW FROM archeological finds that various tribes have been living in what is now Belgium for thousands of years. By 2,000 B.C., Celtic tribes had settled in Belgium and the Netherlands, where they intermarried with Germanic tribes from the north of the Netherlands.

ROMAN RULE

About 50 B.C., when Julius Caesar and his Roman army conquered the area then called Belgian Gaul and stretching from the Seine river to the Rhine river, they had to overcome a group of tribes known as the Belgae. Because the fighting was very fierce, Caesar described the Belgae as the bravest of all the Gauls.

Under the Romans, Belgium became a rich trading center, and in time most people adopted Roman customs. The town of Tongeren grew to be the most important Roman city in the region. It had a big army camp, and strong walls surrounded the city to protect it against foreign invaders.

The Romans stayed for nearly 500 years, but as Roman power declined, tribes of Franks from central Europe settled in the marshy land to the north of the country. In A.D. 496, Clovis I, king of the Franks, defeated the Romans. The Franks spoke a Germanic language, different from the Romanized people of the south, so that even at this early date, the people of Belgium were already divided into two language groups.

It was at this time that Christianity was first brought to Belgium by Irish and Scottish missionaries. They converted Clovis, but it was a second wave of Christianity in the seventh century that had more impact. It was at this time that many of Belgium's great monasteries were founded.

Gent's medieval castle, Gravensteen, is surrounded by thick walls and water to repel invasions.

Opposite: Statue of Godfrey of Bouillon, a Belgian noble and leader in the Holy Crusade.

Even before his death, Charlemagne's brilliant efforts and achievements made him a legendary figure and the subject of veneration in churches. His image is portrayed in Belgium's earliest epic poems and written stories.

FROM TURMOIL TO TRADE

Between A.D. 768 and 814, much of Europe was united under the powerful King Charlemagne and the Belgian area became a very important and prosperous part of the Holy Roman Empire. Being a great organizer, Charlemagne built roads and developed the existing waterways. During his reign, the empire had a well-established intellectual life, and fine arts were encouraged by importing foreign talent.

When Charlemagne died in 814, his kingdom broke apart, and his sons divided their father's empire between France and Lotharingia. The region became more feudalized and suffered the raids of fierce Viking warriors from the north. Nobles lived in fortified castles, and towns built strong walls for protection.

The local counts and dukes became more and more powerful and independent until they were a major force in European politics. When the crusaders sailed off to free the city of Jerusalem from its Muslim rulers, many Belgian nobles gathered their armies and marched with them. Godfrey of Bouillon was one of the leaders at the siege of Jerusalem and was granted the title "Steward and Protector of the Holy Sepulcher."

From the 12th century onward, Belgium started to grow rich from its cloth trade. Belgian cloth was flexible, colorful, and soft and was popular with rich and noble families throughout Europe. Belgium was soon using more wool than it could produce, and merchants traveled to Britain to buy more. Towns such as Ieper, Gent, and Brugge became great trading centers. They sold cloth and metal from south Belgium and bought wool, grain, smoked fish, furs, and timber from all over Europe. Soon the trading activities were regulated by strong guilds. As the merchants became wealthier, they were able to bargain for political rights through charters for their towns and became more and more independent.

BATTLE OF THE GOLDEN SPURS

The Battle of the Golden Spurs took place over 600 years ago but is still an important date for the Flemings in Belgium. At the time, France wanted to take control of the rich lands to its north, and in 1214, the king of France, Philip II, defeated the Flemings and their English allies at the Battle of Bouvines. Over the next hundred years, the French became more powerful in Flanders and, by the 1300s, seemed ready to annex the land and make it part of France.

On the night of May 18, 1302, the citizens of Brugge rebelled, overpowering the guard and murdering everybody they suspected of being French. Encouraged by this news, ordinary people from all over Flanders gathered at Courtrai on July 11, where they defeated the mighty French army in the Battle of the Golden Spurs and saved Flanders from French occupation. At the end of the battle, the Flemings gathered more than 700 golden spurs from dead French noblemen.

THE BURGUNDIAN PERIOD

Although Belgium had prospered, times were still uncertain. Periods of bad weather could bring famines, there was almost continuous warfare, and terrible plagues struck the population, killing thousands of people. During these periods of unrest, the Dukes of Burgundy, who were rich and influential French noblemen, came to power in Belgium. By the early 15th century, they ruled over the 17 provinces that today make up most of Belgium and the Netherlands. Duke Philip the Good is the most famous of the Burgundian rulers. He reigned from 1419 to 1467, extending his domain in battle and improving the economy by reforming tax laws, banning English cloth, and promoting the Antwerp trade fairs.

As the free citizens grew more powerful, they helped pay for the great town halls that are still admired in so many cities today. Rich merchants, the nobility, and the Church started to invest money in art, and a golden age of Flemish painters developed.

The 14th and 15th centuries saw some cities decline and others prosper. Brussels grew into the regional capital for the province of Brabant. The Dukes of Burgundy occasionally held court there, which furthered the growth of the city. The Zwin, an estuary that formed Brugge's access to the sea, silted up, and the city slowly declined. This allowed Antwerp to emerge as a new and dynamic trading center.

SPANISH RULE

When Philip's son, Charles the Bold, was killed in battle in 1477, his daughter Mary married Maximilian of Austria, which brought Burgundian lands under the control of the Hapsburg family. The Hapsburgs were related to nearly all the royal families in Europe, and in 1516, Maximilian's grandson Charles became King of Spain. As a result, Belgium and the northeastern Netherlands became part of the great Spanish empire. Because of heavy taxes, the city of Gent rebelled against Spanish rule. King Charles put down the uprising, but the rebellion continued to simmer. A new religious idea from Germany—Protestantism—added to the unrest. The result was 30 years of war, which ended with the north of the country breaking away from Spanish rule and giving Belgium far more independence.

The medieval glory of Brugge is still evident in the old guildhalls and merchants' houses and the small canals that once linked the city with the North Sea.

In 1659, King Louis XIV assumed power in France. He was determined to make the Spanish Netherlands part of his kingdom. The newly independent Low Countries (Belgium and Netherlands) had to contend with a powerful France as their neighbor, and for the next 50 years, the Spanish Netherlands became a battleground between the Dutch, often aided by other European powers, and the French. In 1695, the French surrounded and bombarded Brussels, destroying much of the ancient city. A series of campaigns led by Britain's Duke of Marlborough and Prince Eugene of Savoy finally forced the French out of the Netherlands.

In the Treaty of Utrecht (1713), France abandoned any claim to the Spanish Netherlands, but this left the European powers with the problem of what to do with the country. They did not think it could survive as an independent nation, so the Spanish Netherlands was given to Charles VI, emperor of Austria, and became known as the Austrian Netherlands.

THE FIGHT FOR INDEPENDENCE

Subsequently, an independence movement arose in Belgium, which the Austrians did their best to suppress. In 1794, Belgium was suddenly annexed by France's new revolutionary government. French rule, particularly under Emperor Napoleon Bonaparte, brought many important changes to the country. Industry was encouraged and the port of Antwerp, which had been closed for many years, reopened. The metric system and a new legal code were introduced, and Belgium was divided into nine departments.

The Brussels Grand Place was the target of French bombardment in 1695. Soon after, the medieval grandeur of its guild houses, with their gilded scrollwork and statues, were restored in a curious mixture of French and Italian Renaissance styles.

THE BATTLE OF WATERLOO

After a series of defeats in 1813 and 1814, Napoleon Bonaparte was exiled to the island of Elba. In 1815, he escaped, regained power in France, and started gathering a new army. Knowing he had to strike first, Napoleon marched into Belgium. On June 16, 1815, he defeated the Prussian army at Ligny. He marched on to meet his old foe, Wellington, who had positioned his 200,000-strong force of English, Belgian, and Dutch troops with over 400 cannons south of Brussels, outside the village of Waterloo.

Napoleon delayed his attack because of rain but then launched his men at Wellington's right flank. This was not supposed to be the main attack, but more and more soldiers were drawn into the battle. In the early afternoon, Napoleon finally launched his main assault on the center of the allied line, but to his surprise found he was now fighting the Prussian army as well. The Prussian army, led by Marshal Blücher, had evaded pursuing French troops and come to Wellington's assistance. Later in the afternoon, the French seemed to be on the verge of victory, but despite a last desperate attack by Napoleon's elite Old Guard, the allied line held firm. With more and more Prussian forces arriving, French hopes faded. Their weary army started to break up and flee south, and Napoleon himself was very nearly captured. Napoleon, who had revolutionized warfare, had fought a strangely unimaginative battle.

The French were never popular, and their defeat in 1814 was generally welcomed. A few months later, Napoleon once again marched into Belgium, only to meet his defeat at the Battle of Waterloo in June 1815.

At the Congress of Vienna in June 1815, the European powers reached decisions over the reorganization of Europe. They particularly wanted to prevent France from further expansion and from ever gaining control of the port of Antwerp. Under the influence of Great Britain and ignoring the wishes of the Belgian people, they united the country with the Netherlands under the reign of William of Orange. In August 1830, a revolution broke out against Dutch rule, and by the end of the year, Belgium had declared independence.

A short period of anarchy followed, during which the new nation had to search for a king. The selection of German Prince Leopold of Saxe-Coburg-Gotha, an uncle of Queen Victoria, received the final approval of the major European powers. King Leopold I ascended the throne on July 21, 1831, the date now recognized as Belgium's independence day.

INDUSTRY AND COLONY

As Europe switched from an agricultural to an industrial economy, Belgium was in the ideal position to benefit. The newly independent nation had excellent harbors, both on the coast and inland, and seemingly endless coal fields. In 1835, the first railway line on the mainland of Europe was opened between Mechelen and Brussels. Equally important, Belgium's neutrality seemed to be accepted.

Leopold II came to the throne in 1865. A keen supporter of industry, he encouraged the construction of many great buildings. Leopold II also believed that Belgium should become a colonial power. He commissioned Henry Stanley to make a second trip to central Africa, and the explorer carried with him treaties,

As a result of the renovations commissioned by King Leopold II, the city of Brussels became known as little Paris.

which he persuaded many local chieftains to sign. Leopold established the Congo Free State (now Zaire) and ruled it as his personal property. The territory prospered, supplying Belgium with rubber, ivory, and other valuable resources. Unfortunately, little of this new prosperity benefited the ordinary people of Congo, who protested their poor wages and harsh working conditions. There were international protests at the treatment of the population. In 1908, the Belgian government took over the running of the colony.

THE VIOLENT CENTURY

For much of the 19th century, Belgium lived under the shadow of its powerful neighbor, France. By the end of the century, it was Germany, newly emerged as a united country, that gave greater concern. In August 1914, German troops demanded the right to march across Belgian soil to attack France, plunging Belgium into World War I. The tiny Belgian army put up a brave fight and even flooded large areas of the countryside to slow down the Germans, while British and French troops were rushed in to help. By October 1914, the German advance was halted, with one small corner of Belgium still unoccupied.

Both sides now dug a line of trenches that stretched from the Belgian coast through France and on to the Swiss border. Neither side could break through this defense system, and the war dragged on from one year to the next. It was a time of great hardship for the Belgians, especially for those trapped in the German-occupied part of the country.

The violent battles of 1915, 1916, and 1917, some of which was fought on Belgian soil, cost millions of lives on both sides without achieving victory for either. The Belgian cities of Ieper and Diksmuide and villages close to the front line were totally destroyed. It was 1918 before the arrival of large numbers of US troops finally helped bring about the Allied victory.

After the war, the right to vote was extended to all Belgian men; women's suffrage was granted in 1948. The new government introduced major social reforms that included reducing the working day to eight hours, reforming taxes, and introducing old-age insurance. Although these changes helped to improve the standard of living for the majority of people, the worldwide Depression of 1929–1931 caused considerable hardship and poverty. The 1930s also brought new political tensions, with the rise of Hitler and the Nazi Party in Germany.

During World War I, the Germans prompted international protest when they executed two women resistance workers accused of helping Allied soldiers escape. British nurse Edith Cavell (above), based in Brussels, was arrested in August 1915 and shot the following month. Gabrielle Petit worked on the escape route and also distributed the secret newspaper, *Libre Belgique*. Ms. Petit was arrested and executed in April 1916.

In May 1940, Belgians woke to find that once again their country had been invaded by the German army. Using tanks and aircraft, the invaders were able to overrun the whole of Belgium in 18 days. This time the occupying army was to stay for five years, and in many ways the occupation was to be even more brutal than in World War I.

A war memorial in front of the town hall in the city of Dinant.

Many Belgians were sent to Germany to work as forced laborers, and the Jewish population suffered terrible persecution. In Belgium, the population had to deal with several problems: a freeze in wages, high inflation, a rationed food supply, and a flourishing black market. The Germans fought resistance operations and bombings with violent counter-terrorist activities.

For Belgium, World War II was a time of great confusion. When King Leopold III surrendered to the Germans soon after their invasion, a German military government was set up. At the same time, Belgian institutions were allowed to function normally, but this situation only worked until the fall of 1940.

The Belgian government sought refuge in France and set up a government-in-exile in London in October 1940. Belgian troops based there continued to fight with the Allies. King Leopold III remained in Belgium for most of the war. His wartime presence there later became a controversial issue, referred to as "the royal question."

The Allies invaded north Europe on June 6, 1944, and by September had started the liberation of Belgium that ended with victory in May 1945.

A postwar Brussels landmark: the Atomium was built in 1958 for a world fair. Representing an atom of iron, it houses a museum and a restaurant.

POSTWAR RECOVERY

Belgium's political life after the war was dominated by the delicate royal question and would polarize around the Walloon-Flemish division of the country. A referendum in 1950 voted for King Leopold's return to the throne: yet many people thought he had collaborated with the Nazis, and the strong feelings on this matter threatened to lead to civil war. As a result, King Leopold III abdicated in favor of his son, Prince Baudouin, who ascended the throne when he was only 20 years old. He reigned for 42 years and gained a very popular reputation as a successful mediator; he was often the moderating link between feuding political parties.

After the war, Belgium took a leading role in European and world affairs. The country joined NATO and the European Coal and Steel Community and became a founding member of the European Economic Community, now called the European Union. The Belgian economy flourished and social conditions improved, but during the 1960s differences between the nation's two major language groups led to serious riots. As a result, the constitution was revised to divide the nation into three cultural communities: Dutch-speaking Flanders, French-speaking Wallonia, and a smaller German-speaking community.

During the late 1970s and the early 1980s, the government faced serious economic problems—rising unemployment, high inflation, and a negative balance of payments—in addition to the ongoing linguistic divisions.

INDEPENDENCE IN AFRICA

After World War II, the Belgian Congo and Rwanda were granted their independence. At first Belgium was reluctant to lose its African empire, but confronted with hostile world opinion and with increasing resistance in the Congo itself, Belgium realized there was really no alternative. Nevertheless, until recently, Belgium continued to provide large-scale financial assistance, and Belgian missionaries and aid-workers remained active.

The Congo gained its independence on June 30, 1960. With its great natural resources, it was hoped that the young nation would become a major African power. Instead, tribal conflict broke out, and the rich mining province of Katanga tried to break away as an independent state. The country became involved in a bitter civil war, and many Belgian citizens who had hoped to stay in Africa were forced to leave.

Western governments put their hopes and support behind President Mobutu. At first he did bring some political stability to the nation. He also changed the name of the country from the Congo to Zaire, to help the population forget the colonial past. Over the years, Zaire became more and more corrupt. Although the government was unable to provide its people with basic services, the president and his family became notorious for their personal wealth, which ran into millions of dollars.

By the 1990s, Zaire appeared to be on the verge of total collapse. Under international pressure, Belgium withdrew its support of President Mobutu. Belgian troops were sent to help evacuate an estimated 11,000 Belgian citizens from the trouble-torn African country.

Rwanda was under Belgian rule from 1919 until 1962. In October 1990, violent riots in Rwanda between the Hutu and Tutsi tribes prompted Belgium to protect some 1,600 Belgian citizens still present in the former colony. When continuous intertribal strife culminated in the country's worst genocide in April 1994, the Belgian government and United Nation troops organized the evacuation of all Belgian civilians from Rwanda.

These experiences in Zaire and Rwanda not only marked the end of Belgium's colonial era but also resulted in Belgium renouncing any post-colonial role in Zaire's and Rwanda's future.

These difficulties caused the fall of several successive governments. A period of stability was achieved when Wilfried Martens became prime minister in 1979. Heading six consecutive coalition governments, Martens concentrated on economic issues rather than the linguistic conflicts. These conflicts led to his resignation in October 1991. Under the new prime minister, Jean-Luc Dehaene, the government reached agreement on the long-running language debate. Constitutional changes were passed in 1993 to make Belgium a federation, giving Wallonia and Flanders considerable autonomy.

GOVERNMENT

BELGIUM IS a constitutional monarchy that consists of a federation of largely autonomous regions and Dutch-, French-, and German-speaking communities.

THE FEDERATION

Linguistic differences between the Wallonia and Flemish regions have led to Belgium's transformation from a single central state to a federal state. Four major reforms, started in 1970, have changed the Belgian constitution and given Brussels, Flanders, Wallonia, and the German region considerable autonomy. In February 1993, sovereignty was alloted to three authorities: the central state, the regions, and the communities. Each administrative level has exclusive powers and does not interfere with the other authorities.

By the November 1995 elections, Flanders, Wallonia, and Brussels will each have an elected parliament and a prime minister. The federal parliaments will take responsibility for planning infrastructure, water, energy, regional road development, and the municipalities within their areas. The language communities, which have been established for many years, will still have responsibility for cultural matters (including broadcasting), education, and health.

The Wallonia Parliament will meet in Namur, but Flanders has established its seat of government in Brussels. This political decision was to remind people that the capital is situated in the northern Flemish part of the country. Therefore Brussels is home to the National Parliament, the Flemish Parliament, and the Brussels Parliament.

The Belgian flag has three vertical stripes in black, yellow, and red. The shape of the flag is unusual, as it is nearly square. On the right is the blue European Union flag with the ring of stars representing member nations.

Opposite: The Palace of Nations in Brussels faces the peaceful Royal Park.

NATIONAL GOVERNMENT

Belgium is a constitutional and hereditary monarchy, so the king is the head of state. However, in practice Belgium is ruled by a parliament. Parliament consists of two houses, the Senate and the Chamber of Representatives. At present, the Chamber of Representatives has 212 members, all of whom are elected. The size of the Senate varies but is usually around 180 members. Of these, 106 are elected by the people, 50 appointed by provincial councils, and 25 elected by the Chamber. A place is also reserved for the heir to the throne.

The National Parliament will be reduced in size after the 1995 elections, when some of its responsibilities will be assumed by the federal parliaments. The Chamber of Representatives will have 150 members, the Senate 71. The National Parliament will remain responsible for foreign policy, the national economy, justice, and defense.

The Belgian Parliament meets in these chambers.

Elections must be staged at least every four years, but, in fact, a Belgian government seldom gets through a full term of office. All Belgians over the age of 18 have the right to vote and are required to do so by law.

New bills, which make the nation's laws, have to be passed by both houses, but it is the Chamber of Representatives that has the larger part to play in this process. The Senate's main task is usually to revise the details.

THE POLITICAL PARTIES

There are three main political groups in Belgium—Christian, Socialist, and Liberal. Each party has two linguistic divisions for Flanders and Wallonia. The Christian groups, the CVP in Flanders and the PSC in Wallonia, generally take moderate views on most subjects. Traditionally, the CVP is the strongest party in Flanders and usually forms coalitions with both Socialists and Liberals. The Socialist Party makes social welfare its key issue and is Wallonia's leading party. The smaller liberal parties—the VLD in Flanders and the Walloon PRL—are particularly concerned with limiting government spending and represent the conservative side of the political spectrum. A number of other small parties include the extreme Vlaams Blok, which campaigns for the expulsion of immigrants, and the ecological parties—ECOLO in Wallonia and AGALEV in Flanders.

LOCAL POLITICS

Belgium is divided into 10 provinces, each with its own directly elected provincial council. Each provincial council elects six members as a permanent deputation to work full time and implement the council's decisions. The provincial councils have considerable power. They can draw up regulations, establish the budget and provincial taxes, oversee the accounts, and generally have responsibility for all matters within the province. However, they cannot ignore the laws made by the higher national and federal governments. Each provincial council has a governor appointed by the king; the governor sees that national laws are followed.

The provinces are divided into nearly 600 municipal boroughs, each with its own elected borough council. Most Belgians have a strong historical sense of local autonomy, and within its small area, each

The ECOLO and AGALEV political parties campaign under the ecological banner. However, Belgians tend to be conservative, and it is difficult to make them change their ways, particularly if it means sacrificing personal comfort. A person might decide not to light fires in the garden as this pollutes the neighborhood, but the same person is likely to drive half a mile to the neighborhood shops to avoid walking.

The Berlaymont Building houses the headquarters of the European Union and is built in a remarkable cross-like form.

borough council also has a great deal of authority. Borough councils settle all matters of local interest, including the budget, accounts, and utility rates. Seeing that their decisions are acted on is the responsibility of the local corporation, which is headed by the burgomaster and the aldermen. The burgomaster is appointed by the king on the advice of the borough council. Aldermen are elected by the borough council from among their own members.

There are nearly 13,000 councillors in Belgium, meaning that one in every 600 people is directly involved in local politics. Most of the councillors are part-time politicians who carry out council business in their spare time.

THE EUROPEAN UNION

Brussels is the home of the European Union (EU), which is becoming an increasingly powerful force in European politics. The EU operates under a system that makes Belgium's government look simple in comparison. Most of the important agreements and decisions are made by the Council of Ministers. Its members are usually the foreign ministers of the member nations, but meetings might involve other ministers, depending on the agenda. Usually the heads of governments meet once or twice a year during the European Council. Decisions reached at these meetings are passed to the European Commission, the executive body with its teams of secretaries, translators, accountants, and everybody

SOVEREIGN POWER

King Baudouin died suddenly in July 1993, after ruling for 42 years. He often acted as a mediator between the two major language groups and enjoyed high popularity. Because his marriage was childless, Baudouin's brother, Prince Albert, became king. Princess Paola is the new queen.

The King of Belgium has many roles. He is the commander-in-chief of the armed forces, appoints and dismisses ministers, summons or dissolves parliament, confirms and signs the new laws, and is involved in the selection and appointment of judges and senior diplomats.

Although his actual royal power is today strictly controlled, the king retains considerable influence. He can be an impartial arbiter in disputes and has almost daily contact with decision-making people in all realms of Belgian life. The king also has the right of veto. In April 1990, the country faced a brief constitutional crisis when King Baudouin felt he could not sign the government's new abortion laws. To solve the problem, the king assumed his "incapacity to rule" status and abdicated from the throne for 36 hours while the laws were passed; he then resumed his position.

else who makes up the "Eurocracy." By issuing reports on the amount of beach pollution, or setting common standards for drinking water, the EU can influence the living standards of the millions of people living within its boundaries.

There is also a European Parliament, with members who are elected. The European Parliament does not have the powers normally associated with parliaments and cannot make laws. Its influence is really limited to posing questions to both the European Commission and the Council of Ministers.

The EU was born in 1958 with just six member nations and at first aimed simply to remove trade tariffs within Europe and create a common market. Now it has grown to 12 members and is bringing the nations of Europe closer in many different areas.

Above: **King Albert and Queen Paola.**

ECONOMY

LIKE ALL EUROPEAN NATIONS, Belgium is facing some serious economic problems, particularly unemployment, a budget deficit, and recession. In late November 1993, after a series of one-day strikes organized by the unions, the country was brought almost to a standstill by a general one-day strike called to protest the government's austerity plans.

Despite these problems, Belgium is still one of the wealthiest countries in the world: it enjoys a stable currency and low inflation, and industry is becoming increasingly modern and competitive. Above all, the population is well educated, and the work force is one of the most productive in the world.

Heavy industries, dependent on coal and iron, have traditionally been at the heart of the nation's wealth. These have declined over the last 20 years, and high-technology industries have become far more important. This has caused dramatic social changes, with a great deal of the nation's wealth switching from Wallonia to the more modernized Flanders.

Being a small country, Belgium has only a limited domestic market, and firms need to sell their goods overseas. Two out of every three of Belgium's industrial workers produce goods for export, and the country exports about 120 million dollars' worth of commodities and services daily. This reliance on exports means that the Belgian economy can be seriously affected by international events. Belgium's main trading partners are France, Germany, the Netherlands, Great Britain, and the United States.

Belgian banknotes and coins.

Opposite: **Glass-making in Wallonia, an industry since the second century.**

35

A metal production plant in Belgium. Metal production in Belgium declined in recent years.

INDUSTRY

Industry employs about 800,000 people and generally involves importing raw materials and exporting finished or semifinished goods. The range of goods Belgium makes is quite remarkable and includes cars, locomotives, textiles, plastics, glass, paints, industrial chemicals, explosives, fertilizers, photographic material, and medical drugs. Belgium is the world's leading manufacturer of carpets and billiard balls, and is known worldwide for its fine crystal glassware.

The last 30 years have brought major changes to Belgian industry, with far-reaching social and political consequences. During the 1960s, the traditional heavy industries, which centered around the Walloon cities of Liège and Charleroi, paid the price of using obsolete methods and started to decline. The textile industry also could no longer compete with products coming from third world countries where wages were far lower.

High-technology industries have grown in importance. These are generally located in modern industrial estates just outside of towns, and include industries such as biotechnology, lasers, microelectronics, office equipment, robotics, medical technology, aerospace, and telecommunications.

Whereas the old industries had depended on the canals and railway lines, these new industries are more concerned with being close to highways. Most also prefer to be in Flanders, closer to port facilities. This trend to move toward the coast is sometimes called maritimization. Today Flanders is responsible for 60% of the nation's GDP, compared with only 25% from Wallonia. The Flemish part of the country accounts for an even larger percentage of exports, producing some 70% of the total.

The old industrial cities are now going through a painful process of modernization, and a few firms that used to register losses are making a comeback as smaller, more streamlined, and profitable businesses. The textile industry has also been able to regain a larger share of the market.

In the 19th century, Belgium was the first country on the European continent to be caught up in the industrial revolution, which began in Great Britain.

RESEARCH

One reason Belgian industry has been so successful in adapting to new trends is that the country has made a big commitment to industrial research. There is talk in Belgium of a third industrial revolution, a collaboration between science and industry.

Research centers include Louvain University, which has undertaken extensive research into human gene technology, and the IMEC center, which works in microelectronics and microchip research. Gent has the Plant Genetic Systems bacteria bank, and Liège is the home of an important space research center. Belgium is also leading the way in laser research.

So far, nine Belgians have won a Nobel Prize, five for science. The most recent winners are Ilya Prigogine, who won the prize for chemistry in 1977, and Albert Claude, who received the prize for medicine and physiology in 1974.

POWER AND TRANSPORTATION

Belgium's industry was traditionally powered by its coal fields. Coal production reached its peak in 1953 when 33 million tons of coal were mined. By the 1980s, that figure was down to seven million, and gas and oil were becoming far more important energy sources. One by one the coal mines were forced to close, causing considerable hardships in the coal-mining communities. The last Walloon coal mine closed in 1984. The Zolder and Beringen mines in the Kempenland region continued operations for several more years, but also closed in 1992. This left the country completely dependent on imported oil and gas.

As a result, Belgium has made a major commitment to nuclear power. The first nuclear power station at Doel, close to Antwerp, opened in 1974. Today there are seven nuclear power stations in operation, and nuclear energy meets 60% of the nation's energy needs. Environmentalists are concerned at the prospect of having so much nuclear activity in such a small country, and in the future Belgium is likely to turn to natural gas for power.

Because of good harbors and an excellent transportation network, Belgium has been described as the gateway to Europe. Antwerp ranks as the fifth largest port in the world and the second largest in Europe; it is also considered to be one of the most efficient ports in the world. Considerable money has gone into expanding other harbors around the country. A new lock on the Gent-Terneuzen Canal will enable larger ships to reach the port of Gent, and the port facilities at Zeebrugge will be expanded by two new harbors. To transport goods to port, Belgium has over 3,000 miles (4,827 kilometers) of railway lines and an extensive road system. Approximately 61% of goods are transported by road and 21% by rail.

Astronauts in space can easily spot Brussels at night, as it sits in the center of a network of well-lit highways.

Although less important than it once was, the Belgian canal system is still used and covers 1,200 miles (1,930 kilometers), linking Gent, Brussels, and Brugge with the sea. The Albert Canal is the country's largest canal. Eighty miles (129 kilometers) long, it was completed in 1939 and links Liège with Antwerp. It is 80 feet (24 meters) deep at the shallowest point, and barges weighing up to 2,000 tons can sail through it.

Airlinks are also important. The Belgian national airline, SABENA, has service to destinations all over the world.

AGRICULTURE AND FISHING

Today farming employs only 3% of the work force, and most farms are family-owned enterprises. The amount of land being used for agriculture is decreasing, but Belgian farmers use extremely modern methods and are actually producing more than ever. This is made possible by factors such as higher quality seeds and plants and soil preparation. Belgian farmers provide one-fifth of the nation's food requirements.

The major crops are sugar beets, potatoes, and wheat, followed by barley, corn, and oats. Much of the grain goes to feed livestock, and cattle are the mainstay of the farming economy. There are about 3.3 million cattle in Belgium, and beef and dairy products form an important part of the Belgian diet. Different regions specialize in different products. The soil in northeastern Ardennes is used only for pasture land, horticulture is encouraged in Gent, and where the soil is sandy, farmers tend to specialize in pig and chicken farming. Recently the market has grown for special crops, such as hops, tobacco, fruit, and flowers.

Fishing is of minor importance to the Belgian economy. Concentrated in Oostende, Zeebrugge, and Nieuwpoort, the industry adds a great deal to the character of these coastal towns. About 95% of the catch consists of fish, with crustaceans and mollusks making up the rest.

Fishing for shrimp along the North Sea coast is still done in a traditional way.

THE WORK FORCE

The population of Belgium is around 10 million people, and about four million are part of the active work force. Women make a considerable contribution to this figure: about 1.5 million women work outside the home.

Today about 70% of the work force is employed in service industries, such as education, transport, the hotel business, banking, and finance. Belgium exports a growing number of services, with Belgian consultants and financial advisors working around the world. Belgians believe that they are good workers who take pride in finishing a job well. The Belgian work force is well trained and is often multilingual, which is the main reason so many foreign companies have invested in the country.

The Belgian government consults closely with workers, and wages and working conditions compare favorably with most other countries. The average work week is 38 hours, and Belgians have four weeks vacation a year.

Not everybody has been able to adapt to the recent economic changes. People in the old industrial areas who do not have qualifications to seek alternative work are facing the prospect of long-term unemployment. A new phenomenon is the sight of Belgians, some of them quite young, begging on the street. There are many factors at work, both economic and social, but it is still a sight few Belgians ever expected to see.

Most of Belgium's working women are employed by the service sector and in light industries, such as food and textile production. About 23% of female workers are employed on a part-time basis.

41

BELGIANS

BELGIUM'S POPULATION of almost 10 million consists of three main communities: the Flemish-speaking, French-speaking, and German-speaking communities.

TWO DIFFERENT PEOPLE

The Flemings and the Walloons make up the majority of Belgians. The Flemings mostly live in the north and speak Flemish, a version of Dutch. They are descendants of the Franks, the Germanic tribes who invaded the country nearly 1,500 years ago. Belgians from Wallonia, or Walloons, mostly live in the south and speak French. They can trace their ancestry back to the Celtic Belgae tribes who were driven back by the Franks.

The Celtic people consisted of many different tribes who shared a common language and originally came from an area of southern Germany between the Rhine and the Upper Danube rivers. They were reputed to be ferocious fighters who ate and drank great amounts. The Celts were Romanized around 100 B.C. and started to integrate with their Roman invaders.

In a general way, there are differences between the Flemings and Walloons. Because of their Celtic origin, people from Wallonia tend to be smaller and darker than the Flemings. In contrast, a typical person from Flanders would be described as tall, blond,

Opposite: **Belgian accordionist. Belgians make it a point to be friendly and enjoy the good life.**

Below: **Belgian children**

Fleming men in the tra-
ditional clothes of farm-
ers, worn for a festival.

*Belgians are less
concerned about
the destiny of
nations than their
own region. A
Belgian is more
attached to the city
that gives his or
her region its
character and to
the countryside.*

and blue-eyed. There are many people who would indeed fit these typical descriptions, but the divisions in Belgian society are really more a matter of language and culture.

Traditionally, the French speakers looked down on their Flemish-speaking neighbors. The Walloons were also the economically dominant group in the country because most heavy industry was located in the south. The Walloons' perception that they speak a sophisticated international language also added to a feeling of superiority. In contrast, the Flemings seemed to suffer from an inferiority complex, due to the localized use of the Flemish language and their less-developed economy.

Later, as the Flemings became a majority in Belgium, they regained confidence. Today Flanders is the stronger of the two economies, which is changing the way the communities regard each other. People in the Flemish region have started to feel that their enterprise is wasted by having to support the economically ailing south.

THE GERMANS—BELGIUM'S THIRD GROUP

About 70,000 people of German background live in a small strip of land around the town of Eupen, close to the German border. They are the third cultural group in Belgium and are acknowledged as a national culture. German was recognized as one of Belgium's official languages in 1963.

This region was given to Belgium by the Treaty of Versailles at the end of World War I. The area was briefly annexed by Germany during World War II and was returned to Belgium after the Allied armies liberated the country in 1944. Immediately after World War II, the Belgian government opened up files on thousands of German Belgians they thought might have collaborated with the Nazis, and many people lost their civic rights.

Today the region is peaceful, and the vast majority of people will probably describe themselves as Belgians who happen to speak German. At the same time, people in this region feel strongly about their German culture and language.

Residents of German-speaking Belgium in front of a German information center.

The German minority have benefited from the ongoing struggle between Belgium's two larger language groups, and they have acquired considerable independence without ever really campaigning for it. There are a German radio station and television service for the area and a few small German newspapers.

Children learn French starting in the first grade and a third language as they grow older. Economically, the area has strong links with Germany. The large German city of Aachen is just across the border, and many people commute there to work.

LES MAROLLES—A WORLD OF ITS OWN

Les Marolles ("LEH mah-ROHL") is the old working-class region of Brussels and consists of the alleyways that lie in the shadow of the Court of Justice. Traditionally, the people living here were employed as low-paid manual workers or were involved in small-scale trading. Like the London Cockneys, the people here developed their own *Marollien* ("mah-roh-LYEAN") dialect and had a special sense of humor. For example, most people hated the giant Court of Justice that towered over their neighborhood, and they managed to turn "architect" into a derogatory remark.

The *Marolles* dialect, a version of French with many Flemish words mixed in, was the result of workers from both language groups living closely together in these narrow streets. The dialect even retained some words from Spanish, a legacy from the days when the soldiers of Philip II roamed the crowded streets.

The unique spirit and culture of the area has virtually died out due to renovations and new building. Probably the only place you will now hear *Marollien* is in the Toone Puppet Show and some cafés. The most vivid legacy of the area is the daily flea market, where tourists and people from all over the city like to meet on sunny mornings.

HOW THE BELGIANS SEE THEMSELVES

There are common characteristics that cross the French-Flemish barrier. Most Belgians consider themselves to be reasonably easygoing and ready to compromise, but at the same time independent and capable of being quite stubborn if the need arises. They are hard workers as well as pleasure-seekers with a passion for good food and varied cultural activities. Many a Belgian will admit that moaning and grumbling is a national characteristic. The ability of the average Belgian to moan about events, but then to forget their problems and carry on, is probably a major reason why Belgium has stayed together as a nation.

This attitude might be a legacy from years of living under foreign rule, when people had to hide their feelings and get on with life as best they

could. Typical is an indifferent attitude toward authority: people joke
that whenever a new law is introduced, Belgians will immediately start
looking for ways around it. This is probably true for many traffic
regulations, and certainly for tax laws. Avoiding paying taxes, either by not
declaring all one's income, or by overclaiming on expenses, is almost a
national hobby and is not really considered immoral.

Having the right connections is also very much part of the Belgian way
of life. For example, until recently it could take up to several months to
have a telephone installed unless you knew somebody working in the
telephone company. Since 1992, the state-owned telecommunications
company has been transformed into an efficiently run enterprise. Finding
work is another area where people who have some influence will often
try to help their friends and relations. People seldom receive money for
doing such services but will expect the favor to be returned at some point.

FOREIGNERS

Belgium's healthy economy attracts many people from other countries. In the 1960s, immigration was encouraged by the government, as Belgium had a shortage of labor. This first wave of immigrants came mainly from Italy and Morocco. Many became Belgian citizens and part of the nation's increasingly mixed community. Others integrated into Belgian society but have chosen to keep their original nationality. Some have taken this option simply to avoid doing national service in Belgium. People from the former African colonies add another dimension to the ethnic mixture.

It is estimated that today 860,000 foreigners live in Belgium, a very significant number for a country where the total population is only just approaching the 10 million mark.

Belgian laws protect the ethnic and religious freedoms of all people, but social and cultural problems remain. Many immigrants have found it difficult to integrate with the rest of the population, and there is a tendency to group together in certain areas of the city. About 28% of the people living in Brussels is of non-European origin, and most foreigners are concentrated in the areas of heavy industry in Wallonia.

Immigrants have no voting rights, and it is not easy for people of non-European origin to find jobs in government service, or at anything other than manual work or production line work. Many have therefore tended

Many ethnic backgrounds are in evidence in the schools of Brussels and the regions with a high concentration of immigrants.

A NEW GENERATION OF IMMIGRANTS

A new generation of children of immigrants is achieving fame in Belgian society. Alida Neslow is a young African Belgian woman who now anchors programs on the Flemish television channel. Elio Di Ruppo (right) is the first Italian Belgian to make any real impact on politics; he became minister of communications and public enterprises in 1991. Rocco Granata, a popular singer, is also of Italian origin. Enzo Scifo, another Italian Belgian, is the star of the national soccer team and became so famous that he went back to Italy to play as one of the foreign players in the Italian professional league.

to gravitate to jobs where they are more welcome. Most of the taxi drivers in Brussels, for example, are originally from North African or Middle Eastern countries. Some immigrants have been very successful in operating their own small businesses.

Children born in Belgium of immigrant families seldom have the problems with language that their parents had, but they can be confused by the different cultures they experience at home and in school. Muslim girls and women in particular have to make important decisions about dress—for instance, they might be under pressure by their families to keep their hair covered either in school or at work.

Recently a new wave of immigrants arrived from Poland and Romania. Many of them work illegally in construction and textile industries, which means they are cheaper to employ than Belgian citizens. This has become a serious problem, and the government had to introduce heavy fines and prison sentences for people employing illegal labor. When caught, illegal immigrants are immediately repatriated to their country of origin.

Many ordinary Belgian citizens see immigration as one of the most important issues in the future of their country. The extreme Vlaams Blok party has taken advantage of this and hold campaigns under the slogan "Our Own People First." Their extreme views won the party 25% of the votes in Antwerp during the 1992 elections. On the other hand, marches in Brussels to call for racial tolerance have attracted over 20,000 supporters.

A significant proportion of the foreigners in Belgium are Eurocrats involved with the European Union or international businesses. They have made a noticeable impact on the local economy. Housing prices in and around Brussels have risen sharply, causing resentment among the local people, few of whom enjoy the same high salaries.

LIFESTYLE

BELGIANS TRADITIONALLY withdraw into small, familiar groups. It is in their own homes and their own communities that they feel the most comfortable. They place great importance on family, friends, neighbors, and food.

HOUSING

Belgians enjoy a high standard of living. Buying, or preferably building, a home is extremely important. They have an expression that sums this up: "Every Belgian is born with a brick in the stomach." Two out of every three Belgians own their own house.

Many Belgians do not like living in cities and prefer to buy a house or an apartment in a smaller town and then commute to work. This has led to more building in the villages and countryside and a growth of suburbs at the edges of cities. Cities have been transformed into office and service areas. The differences between rural and urban lifestyles are diminishing, although it is still true that city dwellers have a more hectic life and are more outgoing than rural dwellers. Rural people value strong family ties and are protective of their quieter and more relaxed way of life.

Most of the houses are single-family houses and are equipped with every modern comfort. If possible, a big garden surrounds the house and is carefully maintained. As privacy is important to Belgians, their homes function as enclosed shelters that are cosily decorated with solid furniture of classical or modern design.

Houses of all styles, modern and classic, mingle throughout the Belgian landscape.

Opposite: **Children on an outing at the Coo water-falls in the south of Belgium.**

There are some marked trends across the country. Flanders has far more new houses than Wallonia, where most of the houses are over 75 years old. In Flanders, more than half the homes were built after World War II. The Belgian desire to build a house has had an impact on the environment. Many Belgians are unhappy that more and more houses are appearing along the roadsides. It is now possible to drive long distances and never see open fields. The same is true along the sea front, where the number of apartment buildings seems to increase every year.

CARS AND CLOTHES: THE IMAGE OF SUCCESS

Belgians respect successful people, and there is considerable social pressure to find good jobs and gain promotion. As Belgians tend to be suspicious of officials in government or high positions, there is often more respect for people who start and run their own business.

Belgian society places particular emphasis on material possessions, and most people feel it is quite important to assert one's status in society. Cars and good clothes are therefore important status symbols. Virtually every family has all the luxuries of modern life. Yet it is estimated that nearly 40% of the population has not been able to put aside any savings, and about half the population does not go away for a vacation.

One out of every two Belgians owns an automobile, and a quarter of the population has a second family car. The type of automobile is very important, as it advertises

Belgians appreciate expensive cars and a formal dress code.

one's wealth and position in society. The way Belgians drive also reflects the feeling of power they get behind the wheel of a car. An automobile that stalls or is slow to start at the traffic lights will get honked at by all the impatient drivers behind, and pedestrians caught crossing the road as the traffic signals change are given similar treatment.

Many people acknowledge that Belgians are not particularly safe drivers. Despite strict laws to make roads safer, there are often bad accidents. Unless the police are in sight, many drivers tend to ignore the minor regulations. Cars weave through traffic at high speeds, even in places where that means rattling over old cobblestoned streets.

If Belgians put less emphasis on clothing than the French or Italians, they still like to look good. Particularly in Brussels, it is evident that people invest a great deal of care and money in their appearance. The clothing budget of most Belgians is spent on good quality apparel. The dress code is quite formal. In offices, men are still expected to wear jackets, although in winter, as a concession to the cold, a jacket might be replaced by a smart wool sweater. It is quite acceptable for women to wear slacks to work.

Fast cars take their toll on Belgium's highways: every year some 600 men and women under 25 years of age die in car accidents. Especially during weekends, young people try to impress their friends by driving recklessly—too often their lives end on the road, in an ambulance, or in the hospital.

53

Having a chat or just watching people go by while sitting on a bench in a village.

SOCIAL INTERACTIONS

Belgians are quite reserved. It would certainly be considered unusual for a stranger to try to strike up a conversation in public. People become even more isolated in winter, when the weather tends to put everybody in a bad mood. When introduced to strangers, Belgians are generally formal and polite, and the conversation usually concerns trivial subjects like the weather, which is a favorite topic of discussion.

Belgians tend to shake hands more than the English, but less than the French. Colleagues greeting each other at the start of another day at work might shake hands in a relaxed way. Between strangers, the handshake is far more formal, and the two parties introduce themselves by simply uttering their surname. Telephone manners are similar: as they lift the receiver, Belgians simply announce their family name.

When relatives meet, they might shake hands, hug, or do some combination of the two. Family members might also exchange kisses on the cheek, once or three times. There are no rules of etiquette to this, people just seem to know what to do. Friends usually greet each other with only a hug or a single kiss on the cheek. Kissing as a greeting might take place between men and women, or between women, but never between men. It is now also common to see young children slapping hands, a habit copied from American movies.

Women who are close friends might walk arm in arm under some circumstances, for example, when strolling along on a holiday. Men would never do so.

FAMILY AND CHILDREN

Due to a low rate of births and deaths, Belgium's population figures have changed over the last few decades, leaving the country with almost zero population growth and an aging population. However, with a population of almost 10 million—nearly 840 inhabitants per square mile (325 per square kilometer)—Belgium is still the second-most-populated country in Europe.

The average family size at the turn of the century was five people. This number declined until World War II. During the postwar baby boom the average family had three children. This number has now dropped to almost two throughout the country, even in the Flemish region, which traditionally had a higher birth rate than the rest of the nation. Another factor is that more men and women choose to stay single or to delay marriage and having children. Divorce, on the other hand, has risen dramatically over the last 15 years.

A family outing on a sunny day along a coastal promenade.

LOOKED AFTER BY THE STATE

Belgium has a highly developed system of social services and spends more on social protection than the European average. The system costs the government almost 35% of the GDP. Belgians receive a family allowance, free education and scholarships for advanced education, health care, pensions, and welfare benefit for the unemployed.

Health care alone accounts for 7% of the gross national budget, and a large proportion of the total is expended on the health of senior citizens. A low birth rate and an excellent health care system have brought a noticeable change in the average age of the population. At the start of this century, one out of every 15 Belgians was over 60. Today the figure is one out of every five. Belgian men can expect to live to an average age of 72, women to 79. The most common causes of death are cancer and heart disease.

The aging of the population has created some serious social and economic problems. The country faces a rising bill for nursing and pensions. In addition, higher unemployment, a lower birth rate, and more single-parent families make the Belgian social protection system weigh heavily on the state budget. A restructuring to moderate costs was begun in 1981. A portion of the health care costs are now chargeable to patients. Welfare payments to the longtime unemployed are being gradually lowered.

Belgian children are expected to work hard in school and are generally thought of as being quite well disciplined. At the same time, Belgian children have become increasingly status conscious; a great deal of importance is attached to having the latest electronic toys and fashionable clothes. Belgians celebrate their birthdays each year. Children's birthdays are usually the occasion for a small party with friends, games, and presents. After the 18th birthday, people attach less significance to the event, but birthdays are still times for the family to come together.

The really big occasion for most children is reaching the age of 12 and attending the Christian ceremony of Holy Communion. Considering how few people go to church, a surprising number of families still want their children to go through this ceremony. For several weeks beforehand, all the children taking Holy Communion receive religious instruction, and then on the big day they parade through the streets to the church.

Most children enjoy the chance to be the center of attention, with the girls wearing long, white dresses and the boys in their smartest clothes. The event is seen as an important stage in growing up, and the children receive presents and gifts from all their relatives. In many ways, it has become more of a big family party than a religious occasion.

Unlike the United States, there is no real tradition for Belgian children to have part-time jobs, although as they get older most will be required to take on some of the tasks around the house. At 18, Belgians can vote, drive, and leave school.

Today, young adults tend to live with their parents until they can afford their own home. They seem to have a good relationship, and there is respect for their parents since the generation gap has become smaller. But where 50 years ago many Belgian families lived in large houses with several generations staying together, young families now prefer to have their own home, as they do all over the Western world.

As a result, senior homes, where the elderly can live and receive health care, are becoming more common in the cities and suburbs. In fact, there is a feeling that Belgian society is a little too quick to send older people to such homes. In the villages, more emphasis is put on building small flats or bungalows for older people. There it is easier for them to enjoy their privacy and maintain friendships and in addition to have the advantages of village services such as health care and home delivery of groceries.

A class of urban poor has arisen in the old industrial cities, with many Belgians facing the prospect of long-term unemployment. Young people increasingly turn to drugs and crime and make cities such as Charleroi unsafe.

Children file past the graffiti-covered wall of their school.

EDUCATION

Both Flanders and Wallonia have their own separate education ministries, and education is given in the regional language. Education is compulsory until the age of 18, and one out of every four students continue their education beyond this point. Schools in Belgium are run by the government or by private organizations, and those run by the latter are usually Catholic schools. Funds for both state and private schools are provided by the government. The curriculum for both primary and secondary education is guided by education inspectors.

Most parents enroll their toddlers in a preschool. At the age of six, children go to primary school: that lasts for six years. Some secondary schools offer a general education leading to high school and university, and others concentrate on technical, vocational, or artistic programs. In the secondary schools, instruction in the other national languages is also given. Belgian children benefit from all kinds of extras, such as field trips and well-stocked libraries. Wednesday afternoon is kept free from lessons, and many Belgian parents arrange for their children to use this time to take part in activities such as dance, music, or sports.

Belgium has a 500-year history of university education, with the Catholic University of Leuven being an international center of learning and research. Today a network of 19 universities and other institutions of higher learning educate some 100,000 students a year. Students have to complete two cycles that last two to three years before being awarded a degree that leads to a professional life. During the last few decades, increased close cooperation with Belgian industries has helped various universities join the world leaders in scientific research and training.

There are long-term fears that schools could face serious financial restraints in the future. In the summer of 1994, there were major demonstrations by students who felt government cuts were impoverishing their education.

Belgian students work on a project with the aid of a computer.

ROLE OF WOMEN

The last few decades have seen a remarkable "feminization" of the work force in Belgium: from 32% in 1970 to 41% in 1993. Laws passed in 1978 guaranteed men and women equal legal and social opportunities, and equal wages for equal work. In practice, these laws are not always respected: women's incomes are still 30% lower than men's, and in 1993, some 15% of women were unemployed compared to 8% of men. Some attitudes have toughened though: claims of sexual harassment or women receiving unfair treatment at work are now taken very seriously.

Most working women in Belgium still have to combine their professional life with the usual tasks at home.

A high percentage of working women is employed in the services and the government sector, and others work in industry and agriculture. Few women make it to the very top positions in government. Only two out of 16 ministers in the government are women. On the other hand, more highly educated women hold positions in the judiciary and diplomacy, and the government campaigns to encourage women to aim for positions as decision-makers and managers in industries, the media, and the business world.

Government policy to enable working women to combine professional and family life is improving: child care helps women return to work quickly if they wish, but it is also possible for mothers to take up to four months leave to care for their babies. Contraceptives and medical guidance are widely available, and abortion became legal in April 1990. However, it would still be unusual for a man to stay home to look after young children. In general, working women still spend more time doing domestic chores than their male working partners: 36 and 22 hours respectively per week.

THE FUTURE

Unemployment is one of the major concerns for many Belgians. Those who have lost their jobs in the old industrial areas and do not have any other qualifications are facing up to the fact that they might be out of work for years. Young people attending university are also worried about finding work. It is now common to obtain degrees in more than one area.

Immigration is another issue that worries many people; there is a widely held view that too many foreigners are coming to live in Belgium. This is reflected in recent election results that gave considerable support to right-wing parties promising to control immigration.

Taxes are the third great concern. Most people object to paying the high taxes imposed by the government. This is evident in the number of general strikes and public demonstrations.

Language remains another issue to be settled. Some people think the creation of a federal system has defused the language question; others think the linguistic regions of Belgium will continue to draw apart.

Crime is less of a worry than in the United States and in other parts of Europe. One reason is that possession of weapons is strictly controlled. But concern over crime is growing, particularly in the older industrial towns and in cities with a large population of immigrants. These areas are feeling the social impact of having a high number of unemployed people.

Immediately after World War II, three out of ten women aged 25–29 years worked outside the home; now it is eight out of ten.

RELIGION

AT THE START of the fifth century, the warlike Franks moved into Belgium and overran most of the Roman settlements there. One of the Frankish leaders, King Clovis, converted to Christianity in the year 496. A Roman Catholic diocese was established at Tongeren, and basilicas were built around the country as the new religion spread.

The seventh century saw Christianity spread more rapidly. During the reign of the Frankish king Charlemagne, many monasteries were built and the Benedictine abbeys became great cultural centers. The clergy was allied with the local nobility. The 11th century has been called the Age of Faith, when people in both Flanders and Wallonia, and indeed in most of Europe, held unquestioning belief in Catholicism.

The next few centuries saw a lot of religious turmoil. In 1517, Martin Luther published his thesis, which sowed the seeds for Protestantism in Europe. During the period of Spanish rule in the Netherlands in the 16th century, Philip II encouraged Jesuit priests to come to the Netherlands to help reinforce the Catholic faith, which they did in a ruthless way. But when Belgium was annexed by France at the time of the French revolution, the Catholic Church was persecuted and many monasteries closed.

In the years after Belgian independence, the Catholic Party, founded in 1884 and allied to the Catholic Church, emerged as one of the three major powers on the political scene. The party was particularly concerned about religious issues, such as the role of the Church in public life. In recent years, however, there has been a drastic decline in church attendance and, with immigration, a considerable growth in other faiths, particularly Islam.

Catholicism enjoyed a religious monopoly for centuries in Belgium, but later had to compete, sometimes bitterly, with other faiths, such as Protestantism.

Opposite: **The Saint Bavo cathedral in Gent.**

63

Grand Romanesque and Gothic churches were built for hundreds of worshipers. Today these spacious buildings are filled only on special occasions.

EMPTY CHURCHES

Today, Belgium still is predominantly a Roman Catholic nation: about 75% of the population are Catholics. In their daily lives, however, religion plays a far smaller part than in the past. Although church attendance is still slightly higher in Flanders than in Wallonia, and higher in villages than in urban communities, few people regularly attend church.

Yet religion continues to play an important part in the nation's culture, and Belgians still turn to the church for the important rituals in their lives. Most marriages still take place in church, as many young people want to make their wedding day a special occasion, with a limousine, a white dress, and all the pomp and ceremony of a traditional wedding. The church also plays a major role in funerals, and when somebody dies, the priest visits the bereaved family, even if its members do not attend church. In addition, Belgium is the last country in northern Europe to have a Catholic monarch, and most of the national holidays are still based on religious occasions, particularly Christmas and Easter.

Many of the schools in Belgium are Catholic schools. Religious instruction is given during normal class hours, and there is likely to be a small service before school, particularly for the younger children. Priests or volunteers from the church community might make occasional visits.

Despite the small congregations, Belgian churches still demonstrate a remarkable vitality. Congregations are involved in a whole range of community activities, and the buildings are well tended as well as decorated inside with candles and flowers. Churches also sponsor considerable missionary work and aid projects around the world.

RELIGIOUS ORDERS

Monasteries, convents, and abbeys, where people can remove themselves from the material world and devote themselves to God, are an important part of Belgian religious life. Although some of the abbeys and monasteries have closed, there are still people who seek the comfort of life in a religious order.

In some convents, nuns live in total seclusion and avoid any contact with the outside world.

From the middle of the 11th century onward, the religious orders owned some of the richest farmland in Belgium. They became profitable commercial concerns. They used their wealth to help the poor and were important patrons of the arts. Many of the monks were themselves magnificent artists who have left wonderful treasures in the form of manuscripts, metalwork, statues, and paintings.

Many different orders are represented in Belgium, but it is the Cistercians who have probably had the greatest impact. In 1098, Robert of Molesme felt that the Benedictines had become too lax; he left with a few followers to found the Cistercian order. (The Cistercians maintain silence except when absolutely necessary.) By the end of the 12th century, the Cistercians had over 500 monasteries. The order emphasized the importance of manual work and had a great impact on farming techniques throughout the country.

Many monasteries became known for their brewing of beers. This was partly for health reasons, as water supplies were

View over the *Begijnhof* at Brugge. The small houses usually form a square with a peaceful garden at the center.

often unsafe to drink, and partly to raise money for rent. The Trappists, who are a branch of the Cistercians, are the most famous beer brewers, and the Carthusians are noted for their special liqueur, chartreuse.

The *Begijnhofs* ("buh-GEYEN-hohfs") were special religious homes where women could enjoy company and security within a religious atmosphere without taking vows. The movement is believed to have been started by Lambert le Begue to help women who had lost husbands and sons in the Crusades. The *Begijnhof* communities consisted of a church, infirmary, weaving center, and small, individual houses. At one point, *Begijnhofs* could be found all over Europe and were famous for their charitable work. Today they survive only in Flanders and are usually occupied by nuns.

THE SAINTS

Several saints played an important role in the early days of Christianity in Belgium, and some of the early saints, such as St. Amandus and his pupil St. Bavo, came from noble families.

St. Servatius was a priest from Armenia. He became bishop of Tongeren and prophesied the invasion of Gaul by the Huns. He went on a pilgrimage to pray for the safety of his flock during the violent time he saw ahead and died of fever on his return to Belgium. **St. Amandus** was Bishop of Bordeaux around the year 400. He founded monasteries and preached throughout Flanders, making such a contribution to the new religion that he became known as "The Apostle of the Belgians." **St. Bavo** was a nobleman from Brabant who, when his wife died, gave away all his possessions and became a monk at Gent. He did a great deal of missionary work in France and Flanders and then became a hermit. **St. Bernard** was born in France and on the death of his mother joined the religious life. With a few followers, he founded Cistercian monasteries that were to have a great influence in Belgium. Bernard laid down very strict rules that drove some people away, but many others were attracted to the new order. As the number of Cistercian monasteries grew, St. Bernard became a very influential figure, with popes and rulers consulting him on important political matters.

PRIESTS

The Belgian Roman Catholic Church is led by the Archbishop of Brussels and Mechelen. The ordinary priests are the ones who have the most contact with people in their everyday lives. Priests conduct the services and give the sermons. They administer the sacraments, hear confessions, and give spiritual direction to their whole community. In rural areas, they can be seen at local events and helping with youth organizations.

Belgian priests, being Roman Catholic, are not permitted to marry, a restriction many people feel is outdated. The rule on marriage is probably a major reason for a serious shortage of priests in Belgium. Because of the shortage, village priests are often expected to look after several villages, making it impossible for them to have the same personal contact with their congregations as their predecessors did a few years ago.

Lay people also play an important part in running the church. Lay people are committed members of the church community who may help in some of the services by reading from the Bible or distributing Holy Communion. Others visit Catholic schools to give religious instruction.

In Flanders it is common to see small street shrines to the Virgin Mary. These shrines are well maintained and sometimes decorated with flowers. It is difficult to tell whether this is a sign of people's religious beliefs, or just pride in making the neighborhood look nice.

The art of stained-glass making developed from the 13th century onward, and the examples in Belgian churches by masters such as Jean Haeck are considered some of the finest in the world.

PILGRIMAGE

Belgium has several pilgrimage sites, the most important one being at the town of Scherpenheuvel, in the province of Brabant. The main pilgrimage to this site occurs on the Sunday after All Saints Day, in November. Some time early in the 16th century, a shepherd was wandering in the fields near Scherpenheuvel, when he found a statue of the Virgin and Christ Child attached to an oak tree. When he tried to remove the statue, he became fixed to the ground. This was taken as a sign that the statue wished to remain there, and a chapel was built to house it. Although the statue was later destroyed, the place remained an important pilgrimage site, and kings often came to pray before going into battle.

Saint Hubert, a little town in the center of the Ardennes, is another pilgrimage site particularly popular with hunters. According to legend, St. Hubert was hunting there when he saw a stag with a shining cross hanging between its antlers. A voice told him to take up missionary work, and he eventually became the Bishop of Liège. Today St. Hubert is the patron saint of hunters. Sick people might make a pilgrimage to the cathedral at Halle, a small city south of Brussels, which has a black Madonna statue believed to work miracles for people who pray before it.

LIVING MUSEUMS

Over the years, a great deal of energy has gone into building and decorating Belgium's churches and cathedrals; today they are guardians of a considerable national heritage. Although primarily religious buildings, they are also recognized as cultural centers for different forms of expression. Many of the treasures from the very earliest days of Christian history have been lost, but a few wonderful handwritten Bibles, some decorated in ivory and gold, have survived.

The 1400s were noted for the great works of Flemish artists, many of which were commissioned for churches. Probably the most wonderful example is *Gent Altarpiece* painted by Jan and Hubert Van Eyck for the Cathedral of Bavon in Gent. The Antwerp Cathedral has a later but equally impressive treasure in two magnificent paintings by Peter Paul Rubens.

The buildings are also part of the nation's architectural legacy. For the first thousand years of Christianity in Belgium, churches were built in Romanesque style. These were squat buildings with small windows and thick walls that bore all the weight of the structure. In 1242, work started on rebuilding the Cathedral of Notre Dame in Tournai. This was the first time that the Gothic style, which had developed in France, was used in Belgium. By employing buttresses and vaulted roofs, churches attained new height and splendor—vast windows flooded the buildings with light. Over the next century, work started on many of the great cathedrals that still stand in Belgium.

Beautifully decorated churches are often put to good use for concerts of both religious and lay music. Pieces that feature wind instruments, such as trumpets, clarinets, horns, and organs, are particularly effective for the quality of the sound in the high Gothic cathedrals.

OTHER RELIGIONS AND SECULARISM

There are about 250,000 Muslims in Belgium, many of Turkish or North African origins; they are the second largest religious community, as well as the fastest growing ethnic group. The main mosque in Brussels forms the center of the Islamic faith in Belgium. This is an active center, with a school and many other activities related to Islam.

Several Protestant faiths also have a small following among 1% of the population. The main Protestant churches include the Belgian Evangelical Lutheran, the Church of England, and various Free Churches and sects like Jehovah's Witnesses. The Protestant religion in Belgium often has a strong Dutch influence. Generally, the Protestant churches are liberal and are more interested in tending to the needs of their own community than converting people to their faith.

The Jewish population in Belgium is small, around 35,000; this is only half the size it was before World War II. Today Jews largely live in Antwerp and Brussels. The Jewish community includes Orthodox, Conservative, and Reformed congregations.

In the 16th and 17th centuries in the Western world, an important movement proclaiming freedom of thinking and inquiry through scientific and philosophical research developed. As this was a system of social ethics determined without reference to religion, the church defined it as secularism. It gave rise to many ideas in the 19th and 20th centuries, such as positivism, evolutionism, scientism, Marxism, Freudianism, and Existentialism. Some 12% of Belgians declare themselves as free-thinkers— a diverse and pluralistic group from atheists and agnostics to humanists and deists. The Freemasons are the most established group.

In the quiet, green Ardennes forests, the Hare Krishna sect has its own center of faith and learning. Its faith is based on Hindu scriptures, and its robed followers can be seen in the cities selling leaflets.

THE HOLOCAUST YEARS

German troops occupied Belgium in 1940. Life became very hard for everybody. Initially the Jews were not persecuted, but in June 1942 things started to change: they were forced to wear the Star of David on their clothes, which immediately identified them as being Jewish.

That summer the Germans asked for Jewish volunteers to go off to work in labor camps. As the daily conditions of life in Belgium were very severe, many people, believing the German propaganda, thought they might be better off in the camps. The work camps were really concentration camps where the inmates were cruelly treated and then horribly murdered. As frightening rumors spread back to Belgium, the number of volunteers dried up, and the Germans started to hunt down the remnants of the Jewish population.

Many Belgians showed great bravery in helping Jewish families hide, and an underground movement was set up to offer information, money, and the vital ration card. Special effort went into hiding Jewish children. They often had to be isolated from their families and sent to boarding schools, convents, or to live with other families. This was a very traumatic experience, particularly as they had to change their names and never knew where their parents were. After the war, many Jews, mainly in Antwerp and Brussels, started searching for surviving deportees and investigating the whereabouts of disappeared family members.

In Belgium, the somber remains of the Nazi acts are still apparent in a small concentration camp, called Fort Breendonk, near Antwerp. From this fort, thousands of Jews were registered and deported to the German camps.

LANGUAGE

BELGIUM IS LARGELY made up of two groups of people that speak different languages. The Flemings dominate the north of the country and speak Flemish, a version of Dutch. In the south, the great majority of people speak French. In eastern Belgium, near the German border, a small community speaks German.

THE LANGUAGE BARRIER

Long before the modern country of Belgium was created, this small area of Europe was already divided between different language groups. At the fall of the Roman empire, the Frankish tribes speaking a Germanic language moved into the north of the country, and the Romanized and Latin-speaking Celts fled to the south. The language division that exists today was really formed by the collapse of Charlemagne's empire, which formed a "language border." Ever since then, language and politics have always gone hand in hand in Belgium.

When the Burgundian nobles rose to power, French became the language of the court, and therefore of government and power. When the Spaniards faced revolution in their northern territories, they responded by burning Flemish books. Three centuries later, William I attempted to impose Dutch as the official language throughout the Low Countries. That proved to be a bad mistake that ended in general rebellion. Language was also one of the major factors that led to revolution and Belgium breaking away from the Netherlands.

The new constitution signed in 1831 promised linguistic equality, but in practice it was still a great advantage to speak French. Not only did

From 1814 onward, King William I ruled over the Dutch-speaking Netherlands, comprising the present-day Netherlands, Belgium, and Luxembourg. Belgium became independent in 1831.

Opposite: **This bookshop in a beautiful old Brussels arcade sells new and second-hand books in the three national languages.**

73

French speakers still occupy the best jobs, but the language was also thought of as being more refined: Flemish was considered the language of farmers and laborers. As a result, many middle-class people of Flemish background chose to speak French because it was fashionable. This trend was reflected in education, the best private schools teaching in French.

The revival of Flemish was largely inspired by Hendrik Conscience and his wonderful book, *The Lion of Flanders*, which was published in 1838. It demonstrated that Flemish could be a powerful literary language and inspired the campaign for *taalvrijheid* ("TAAHL-vreye-heyet"—freedom of language), the right to use Flemish in official dealings. Laws passed in 1898 gave both languages equal status. However, as the country industrialized, much of the economic activity was based in French-speaking Wallonia, which added more power to the French part of the country.

The use of the three official languages in Belgium is dictated by the linguistic areas in which the country has been divided.

Until quite recently, French has always been the main language of commerce, politics, and management. This meant also that French people traditionally held the top positions in government and business. In fact, one usually had to speak French to get the best jobs, even if one lived in the Flemish part of the country.

The German occupation of Belgium in 1914 saw a few Flemish groups campaign for a separate country under German protection, provoking considerable anti-Flemish feelings after the war. At that time, Belgium was forming far closer political links to France. This in turn

NETHERLANDS

GERMANY

Brussels

BELGIUM

FRANCE

LUXEMBOURG

SPEECH AREAS

■ Flemish (Dutch)   □ German

□ Walloon (French)   ▨ Bilingual Area (Flemish-Walloon)

In the 1960s, violent demonstrations of Flemings versus Walloons in Brussels prompted the government to find a solution to the language problem and avoid a simmering civil war.

caused considerable unrest in the universities. By the 1930s, it was ruled that courts and schools should use the language of their area.

The 1960s brought the language question back as a prime issue. An official language frontier was formed in 1962, but Flemings, believing they were still at a disadvantage, became more determined and occasionally violent in their protests. To solve the never-ending linguistic problems, Belgium decided to form French, Flemish, and German Communities to oversee cultural affairs within their regions. Many of the past prejudices have now been corrected, and the trend at the moment is for peaceful and parallel development—with the different language regions acquiring considerable autonomy from the central government.

Yet language remains one of the major issues in Belgium today, and some people even think the language question could eventually split the nation into two. Recently the Flemish daily *De Standaard* predicted that "It may take a decade, or a generation, but the Belgium state is dissolving itself." At the moment that seems highly unlikely, but all the differences have not yet been totally resolved.

SPOKEN AND WRITTEN LANGUAGES

People in the north of Belgium mostly speak Flemish. For all practical purposes, Flemish is identical to Dutch, spoken in the Netherlands. Only local variations mark the distinction between the two languages, similar to the differences between varieties of English used in Great Britain and the United States. The language can generally be referred to as Netherlandic and belongs to the West Germanic language group. When the language is written, the differences disappear, and Flemish and Dutch are virtually identical.

One interesting difference is that the Dutch have adopted more English and French words into their vocabulary, particularly for technical subjects. Belgian speakers tend to find a Flemish word wherever possible.

People in the south of Belgium happily admit that they speak French. Here as well, the language varies slightly from that spoken in France. Belgians often make French people smile when they talk. To French ears, the French spoken in Belgium can seem unattractive and hard. Standard French is used in both speaking and writing.

Brussels is in a unique position. Geographically it is in the Flemish part of the country, but French has always been more widely spoken within the city. Officially it is now a bilingual city, but in practice French

Live advertising for a Flemish newspaper during the summer holidays at the Belgian coast.

is still more likely to be used than Flemish. Yet Belgians living in the capital easily switch from Flemish to French in their daily conversations.

ACCENTS AND DIALECTS

Historically, Belgium was a collection of city states, and this has had a certain influence on life today. One result is the wide range of local accents and dialects. They can be very limited in extent and range, not only from province to province but also from town to town and sometimes even from village to village.

In the tourist areas of Belgium, signs advertise in Flemish, French, German, and English.

Belgians easily locate each other by their accents and dialects. Some of them are very close to the standard languages used in Belgium, while others include a local patois that is often very distinctive.

In Flanders, the strongest accents are probably those of Limburg and Oostende. Some Flemish speakers find them difficult to understand. In Wallonia, the Liège and Namur accents are also quite particular.

Differences are apparent not only in the way the language is pronounced but also in the vocabulary. For example, the old fishing community in Oostende has hundreds of words and expressions that are unique to the area. The accents remain an active part of Belgian culture, although some of the more extreme versions are now dying out.

In Wallonia a series of local French dialects of Latin origin and influenced by the Celtic and Germanic languages are collectively known as *Wallon* ("wah-LOHN"). They are still spoken, to a limited extent, and have contributed largely to the local dialect-based literature and drama.

LANGUAGE AND DAILY LIFE

The language split has many practical implications for Belgian life. For instance, the media, road signs, and government services have to cater to three language communities.

The state-owned television and radio station broadcasts in Flemish, French, and German. Newspapers address the different communities in their respective languages. So do ministers and other public figures during official functions. The Belgian hospitals, schools, and police forces use one of the three languages, depending on their location in the country.

"Welcome to the village"—signboards or advertisements in the Brussels region often use both French and Flemish.

Most towns are known by their French and Flemish names. A signpost in Wallonia guides you to Bruges, but this becomes Brugge in Flanders. Road signs in and around Brussels, put up by the central government, are in both languages. Some names are easy to identify in either language: Oostende is Ostende and Brussels is Bruxelles in French; Hasselt stays Hasselt. For other names it can be confusing: Antwerp becomes Anvers in French, Liège is Luik in Flemish, and Courtrai is French for Kortrijk.

The language question seldom causes serious problems between individuals on a personal level. A Fleming caught speeding in Wallonia is probably going to be treated just the same as a French speaker. Whether or not they receive a fine or just a warning will depend on all kinds of factors, but language will probably not be a major influence.

NAMES

Belgian surnames are clues to the part of the country people come from. It is a reasonable guess that anybody with a name like *van Damme* or *De Wilde* is from the northern, Flemish part of the country. Similarly, *Delvaux* and *Lefèvre* suggest a Walloon origin. The most common surname of all is probably *Vandeberghe*, versions of which can be traced back to the start of the 13th century. Other common surnames in Belgium include *Janssens, Vermeulen, Lemaitre, Peeters, de Bruyne, Dupont,* and *Roelants.*

It is usual for Belgian children to be given three Christian names, although only the first will generally be used. Traditionally, the

other two are the names of the godfather and godmother. Most boys' names have a Flemish and French version. For example, *Jan* and *Piet* in Flemish translate to *Jean* and *Pierre* in French. Girls' names often cross the language divide, as with *Anne, Carine,* and *Marie.* Television and popular public figures also have a considerable influence on new names, and sometimes names become fashionable at some time or other for no special reason.

THE BELGIAN POLYGLOTS

Historically, Belgium has always had to deal with its European neighbors. As a result, it is natural for Belgians to speak a second or third language or even more, and this trend continues today.

It is required that all children in Belgium learn a second language. In Brussels, a bilingual city, those languages must be Flemish and French, but elsewhere in the country the second language is more likely to be German, English, Spanish, or Italian. German and English are the most popular second languages. English is important as a language of advanced study, and as Germany is both a close neighbor and a major trading partner, German is an important language of commerce. Generally, Flemings seem more open to learning another language. They are certainly more likely to speak French than a person from Wallonia is to speak Flemish.

ARTS

BELGIUM HAS AN ACTIVE and exciting art scene, and a new wave of Belgian artists is attracting headlines in areas such as dance, fashion design, and music. Yet it is inaccurate to speak of a Belgian culture in exactly the same way as one does about a Japanese or a Russian culture, because the work of most Belgian artists is influenced and determined by their French or Flemish backgrounds.

Earlier this century, however, the work of artists such as the painter James Ensor and the composer César Franck started to develop a national feeling, sometimes called *La Belgitude* ("LAH behl-ji-TUU-duh"). There was also a generation of writers who wrote in French but whose stories drew from the history and culture of Flanders. As the language question became more important, it started to have a major influence on the world of art. In the 1960s, the formation of separate ministries of education and culture widened the division between the Walloon and Flemish cultures.

James Ensor's largest and most famous canvas, *Entrance of Christ into Brussels*, painted in 1888, is characteristic of his genius.

Opposite: The opera house in Brussels has recently being revamped into a leading cultural center. It stages great operas and houses Anne Theresa De Keersmaeker's dance company, which is internationally known.

Today French-speaking people tend to follow trends in France. This might include the books they read, the plays they watch, and the music they listen to. Many of Belgium's best French-speaking artists have also tended to move to France, in particular Paris, where they find the art scene more stimulating. The Flemish-speaking community has always appeared more interested in forging its own cultural identity and is not particularly influenced by events in the Netherlands. Nevertheless, the proximity of the German and Anglo-Saxon cultures do play a role.

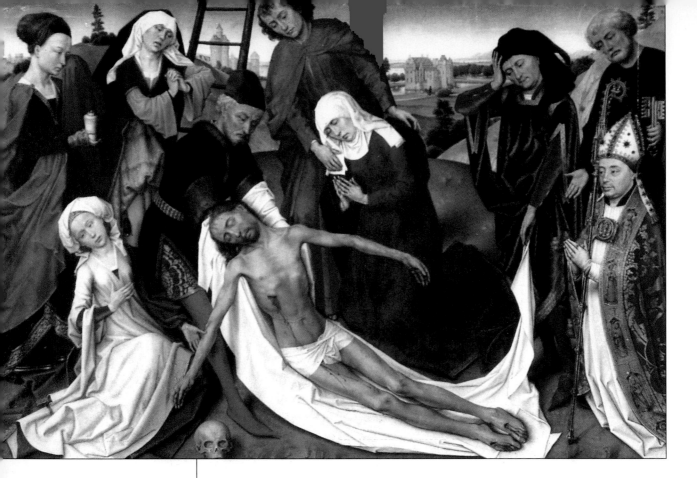

THE RICH PAST

Belgium has a rich artistic legacy, and paintings of the Flemish masters form one of the nation's greatest treasures. During the 15th century, the rich trading cities, particularly Brugge, were able to support many artists. Perhaps the most famous were the Van Eyck brothers, Jan and Hubert. They spent a long period in Brugge, where they developed new techniques of oil painting that allowed them to add far more detail to their work than had been possible before.

Successful artists of the period were usually commissioned to paint for the church or nobility. Therefore most paintings of this period are either portraits or religious scenes, which were painted onto panels to decorate the altars in churches. The Van Eycks' *Gent Altarpiece* is considered to be the greatest masterpiece of this period.

The second half of the 15th century is best remembered for the work of Hans Memling. He settled in Brugge in 1465 and, despite the fact that the economy of the city was declining, managed to win important commissions. His paintings are admired for their beautiful detail.

Hieronymus Bosch was painting during the same period, and his work was very different from the work of any other artist of that time. He painted scenes of the afterlife with bizarre creatures afflicting terrible punishments on sinners. His work was really a form of surrealism, although it was to be several more centuries before that term was first used.

The start of the 16th century saw the end of the early Flemish period. Paintings now covered a far wider range of subjects, including group portraits, landscapes, and still lifes. The great Flemish master of this period was Pieter Bruegel the Elder. He made numerous trips to the countryside to paint scenes of peasant life and gave an excellent idea of what life was like in this period. His famous painting, *Census at Bethlehem,* shows Joseph and Mary on their donkey arriving at the inn, the scene set in 16th century Flanders.

The Peasant Wedding: Pieter Bruegel's impression of medieval rustic life in Flanders' countryside.

The greatest Flemish painter of the 17th century was Peter Paul Rubens, who was born about eight years after Bruegel died. Like many artists of the time, he visited Italy and stayed there for eight years. On his return, he produced an astonishing amount of work, ranging from giant altarpieces to portraits. Toward the end of his life, Rubens retired to the countryside, where he started to paint landscapes for the first time. His work was imaginative and sensuous and brought a new dimension to European painting. At that time, Belgium and the Netherlands were breaking into two separate nations, and Rubens in the south and Rembrandt in the north established new styles of art for each country.

Tapestry weaving flourished in the 15th and 16th centuries, and Belgium's large tapestries were considered to be the best in the world; they hung in palaces, churches, and noble homes all over Europe. The tapestries illustrated scenes from mythology, hunting, tales of chivalry, or Bible stories. The town of Oudenaarde specialized in "green" tapestries using patterns of leaves and plants.

The designs were created by the best artists, and even Rubens once worked on a special design for the Vatican. Once the design was drawn, teams of five or six workers did the embroidery, using colored threads made from wool or silk. Gold and silver threads were also used.

Belgian tapestries can be seen in museums around the country, and a special tapestry museum is located in Tournai. The Royal Tapestry Manufacturers in Mechelen and some individual artists still keep the old skills alive.

The tapestry museum in Tournai. Skilled workers would spend days on finishing a few inches of a pattern.

MODERN PAINTERS

At the end of the 19th century, the enigmatic Symbolist movement provided painters such as Fernand Khnopff and Léon Spilliaert with new inspiration, but it was James Ensor's genuine use of light, masks, and hybrid forms that inspired many later artists.

The surrealist movement produced two world-famous modern painters, René Magritte and Paul Delvaux, and had the strongest influence on modern Belgian painting. Magritte's work is full of fascinating and strange ideas. Leaves turn into trees, trees into birds, and a gray mountainside is, at the same time, a great eagle. One of his most famous paintings is *L'Empire des Lumières*, which he painted in 1954. Paul Delvaux was fascinated by trains and the Brussels trams. These often appear in his work as dark and sinister objects. Motionless nude figures with empty eyes in the foreground of his paintings form the motif in all of Delvaux's work.

In his paintings, René Magritte experimented with a curious mixture of ordinary and strange images.

Around 1950, young artists from Copenhagen, Brussels, and Amsterdam had the desire to rediscover the source of painting and formed the Cobra movement with this objective. Their work often seems strangely childlike and simple, but the group is highly respected and much of their work is now in museums.

Belgian art lovers see art as a good investment, and exhibitions and galleries are thriving. Each year, the Young Belgian Painting movement organizes a well-known art fair with award-winning competitions for modern artists under 40. Here promising artists are discovered by well-known art galleries. Both commerce and the state are important sponsors of art. The Banque Bruxelles Lambert has built up one of the nation's best modern art collections. The state encourages artists by giving out grants to work on public buildings. The Brussels subway stations are the most famous examples.

ARCHITECTURE

The Belgian landscape provides a rich view of its architectural history. Churches and cathedrals in the Romanesque style remain in Tournai and Liège. The great imaginative splendor of the Gothic era is embodied in the cathedrals of Gent, Antwerp, and Mechelen, in the merchants' houses of Brugge, and in belfries and trading halls all over the country.

Horta's private house, carefully restored as the Horta Museum, is one of the last examples of the more than 60 buildings that changed the architectural outlook of Brussels in the early 20th century.

The Art Nouveau movement influenced architecture at the end of the 19th century and the beginning of the 20th. The movement introduced a totally new style, with fluid spiral lines and natural curls, and drew its inspiration from the Japanese, Celtic, and Turkish arts and the observation of nature. The strong sense for detail and beauty turned the movement into a highly decorative style. With architects Victor Horta and Henry Van de Velde, Brussels could have boasted the most beautiful Art Nouveau treasures in Europe if it were not for a careless monument protection policy and the demolition ball that swept through most cities in the 1960s and 1970s.

MUSIC

As early as the 15th century, Belgium was famous for its choirs, which sang in four-part harmony. Belgian composers became famous in the princely churches and chapels of Rome, Milan, and Munich, and musicians came from all over Europe hoping to learn the secrets of the Flemish sound. As the Baroque style developed at the end of the 16th century, Belgian musicians lost favor.

Music took on new life in the 19th century with composers César Franck and Peter Benoit. Under the influence of Benoit and a group of young composers, Flemish music schools in Brussels, Gent, and Antwerp flourished.

Belgium does a great deal to encourage musicians. There are several major national competitions, as well as important international musical festivals that include classical, jazz, or popular music. The world-reputed International Queen Elizabeth Contest focuses on piano and violin in alternating years and attracts contestants from around the globe.

LITERATURE

Literature, more than any other art form in Belgium, has been affected by the country's linguistic problems. Yet, the two literary communities have followed similar paths even as they developed their individual characteristics.

Flemish literature owes a great legacy to Guido Gezelle and Hendrik Conscience. Gezelle was born in Brugge in 1830. Writing poetry of great lyrical purity and of religious and Flemish nationalistic inspiration, this Flemish priest is considered one of the masters of modern European lyric poetry. It is said of Hendrik Conscience that he "taught his people to read." His story, *The Lion of Flanders* (1838), said to be the first Flemish novel, was characterized by Romantic inspiration and national consciousness.

At the turn of the century, a group of writers called *Van Nu en Straks* (Today and Tomorrow) published a review that hoped to gain more recognition in Europe for Flemish literature. Cyriel Buysse, Stijn Streuvels, and Herman Teirlinck were the major contributors. Many of the group were influenced by Guido Gezelle. During World War I, young authors such as Felix Timmermans and Paul Van Ostaijen identified with the German Expressionist movement that was striving for peace and humanitarianism. Van Ostaijen turned later to the nihilistic Dada movement.

Postwar literature was characterized by novelists of different styles and influences, including the magic-realistic novels of Johan Daisne and Hubert Lampo, the socialist-existentialist novels of Louis Paul Boon, and new avant-garde groups. Among them, Hugo Claus became the predominant Flemish writer and is even considered a likely candidate for a Nobel Prize in literature. His novels, poems, and dramas often examine controversial subjects, such as collaboration with the Nazis during the war.

French-language authors—and even French-speaking authors of Flemish origin—produced many outstanding literary works before the independence of Belgium. French-Belgian literature found its own expression only after 1830. In 1867, Charles de Coster wrote *Thyl Ulenspiegel,* which demonstrated how a French language book could have deep roots in Flanders' culture.

In 1881, Max Waller founded the *Jeune Belgique* movement, which attracted a group of young poets and novelists who were engaged in a search for identity: Camille Lemonnier, Eugène Demolder, Georges Virrès, and Georges Rodenbach. Soon a new generation of French-speaking Flemings played a key role in the history of Belgian writing with three poets of international renown: Emile Verhaeren, Max Elskamp, and Maurice Maeterlinck, who won the Nobel Prize in Literature in 1911 for his dramas. His *Pelléas et Mélisande* was arranged into a major opera by the French composer Claude Debussy.

During and between the two World Wars, Belgian literature in French continued to flourish. Novels, poetry, and drama were characterized by stylistic experiments influenced by new avant-garde techniques. Franz Hellens wrote fantastic and mysterious novels, Charles Plisnier's satyric novels won the French Prix Goncourt, and Clément Pansaers' subversive poetry linked the Paris and Zurich Dada movements. Interaction with the Paris literary scene was strong, and a number of Belgian writers moved to that city. So did Henri Michaux, one of the greatest poets of the 20th century, and Georges Simenon, who won fame with his great detective character, Maigret, and his detective stories set in Paris.

Women have always been prominent in Belgium's French language literature. Authors such as Marie Gevers, Suzanne Lilar, and Françoise Mallet-Joris covered different literary styles from novels to essays. Marguerite Yourcenar was the first woman to be elected to the Académie Française.

Georges Simenon was a prolific author. He wrote some 400 books that inspired 54 movies and over 200 television plays.

FOREIGN WRITERS IN BELGIUM

Belgium, and particularly Brussels, has attracted many great foreign writers. Charlotte Brönte visited Brussels in 1842 to learn French. She later came back to work as a teacher, and her books *Villette* and *The Professor* give wonderful descriptions of the old Brussels.

Lord Byron passed through to visit the battlefield of Waterloo. He is rumored to have vandalized one of the statues in the city center, and a minor financial scandal caused him to leave town rather quickly.

When exiled from France, Victor Hugo stayed several years in Brussels while working on *Les Misérables*.

Perhaps the most famous Belgian character to appear in any book is the detective Hercule Poirot. His character was created by the English author Agatha Christie.

CINEMA

Cinema is another field in which Belgium has a certain renown and where both major linguistic communities seem to find a common cultural identity. Despite the difficulties of public funding and the competition with the neighboring French film industry and the bigger international film production companies, Belgian directors have succeeded in producing original films of great quality. Stijn Coninckx was nominated for an Oscar in 1993 for his social drama *Daens,* filmed in Flemish. Chantal Akerman's French-language films are screened in most French-speaking countries.

Belgian filmmakers use both Flemish and French, or they use English as the common—and more international—language. Some also make ample use of local dialects.

André Delvaux, probably Belgium's most famous filmmaker, directed his films in both Flemish and French and adapted novels of Flemish and Belgian-French origin. Other filmmakers, such as Marc Didden and Dominique Deruddere, who won international fame with his full-length film *Crazy Love,* film directly in English. Marion Hansel's film, *Dust,* which won the Silver Bear at the 1985 Venice Film Festival, was also filmed in English.

DRAMA AND DANCE

Although Belgian theater and dance companies generally struggle with low budgets, they have a reputation for staging excellent productions. Many of the companies perform extensively abroad and have won international awards. Theatrical life in Belgium today is blooming with an increasing number of quality companies. Theater and dance festivals, which stage local and international companies, enjoy high attendance.

Theaters in Brussels and Wallonia stage the work of playwrights such as Maurice Maeterlinck, Michel de Ghelderode, Suzanne Lilar, and contemporary writers Liliane Wouters and Jean-Marie Piemme. A major international repertoire has also been adapted, from Samuel Beckett and Dario Fo to William Shakespeare.

In Flanders, theatrical activity is mainly concentrated in Brussels, Gent, and Antwerp. Theater production here is most influenced by the work of playwright, poet, and novelist Hugo Claus, who also directed the theater group in his hometown of Gent.

In addition, strong local actors and directors have searched for new forms of expression that have led some companies to make links between theater, dance, and film. The internationally known works of Jan Fabre and Wim Vandekeybus are examples of the new forms.

Wim Vandekeybus's company at work. His fascinating performances include dancers, blind actors, and live music.

CARTOONS

Cartoons make a particularly important contribution to Belgium's culture. By far the most popular is Tin Tin, the young reporter with his dog Snowy and his friend, Captain Haddock. Created by cartoonist Hergé, Tin Tin first appeared in newspapers in 1929 in an adventure called *Tin Tin in the Land of the Soviets*. Since then his adventures have taken him all over the world, and even to the moon. In Belgium and much of Europe, Tin Tin is as famous as Snoopy and Garfield are in the United States. In fact, General de Gaulle, the late president of France, once said Tin Tin was the only person in the world more famous than he was!

Other famous Belgian cartoons include *Spirou, Marsupilami*, and *Lucky Luke*. Spirou is a hotel bellboy who has a series of exciting and comical adventures. Lucky Luke is a cowboy with a faithful horse, Jolly Jumper, and Marsupilami is a strange spotted animal from outer space.

Cartoon films have also been successful

in the Belgian and international film industries. The rather earthy but very humorous films by Brussels' humorist Picha have been screened all over the world, and Raoul Servais and Nicole Van Goethem, from Gent and Antwerp, respectively, have won several international prizes.

For almost three decades, the Brussels opera *Théâtre de la Monnaie* was home to Maurice Béjart's *Ballet du XXème Siècle*. Béjart, long a symbol of the modern Belgian dance scene, is known worldwide. His ballet school *Mudra* has revived the Belgian dance tradition and trained many dancers and choreographers. Under Béjart's influence and in reaction to his style, other young advocates of modern dance, such as Anne Theresa De Keersmaeker and Michèle Anne Demey, have made their mark on international stages.

FAMOUS LACEMAKING

Lacemaking has a special place in Belgian folklore. The tradition is especially strong in Brussels and the surrounding Brabant countryside. Lace first became popular in the 16th century, when rich men and women wore it to decorate their clothing and to demonstrate their wealth.

Brussels lace was particularly prized, as it both was finely made and used interesting designs. At the height of the fashion for lace in the 17th and 18th centuries, the industry employed thousands of women, giving them an important source of extra income.

The economic importance of lacemaking became quite a political issue. At one point, the British government became worried about how much money was being spent on Belgian lace, and they tried to ban its import. Emperor Philip II of Belgium tried to prevent girls over 12 from working in the industry, as it had become difficult to find anybody willing to work as servants. Neither ruler had much success with these campaigns. Eventually wearing lace simply went out of fashion.

The professional lace-makers are trained from childhood and produce the finest designs following traditional patterns.

Today tourism and a growing interest in the past have revived interest in lacemaking, and many Belgian women have started learning and practicing the art, both as a hobby and as a source of extra income. Most of the lace, usually tablecloths and blouses, finds its way to tourist shops in Brugge and Brussels. Because of the work involved and the high cost of labor in Belgium, lace is expensive. A large tablecloth costs around $230.

LEISURE

WITH A FIVE-DAY working week of 38 hours, some 10 official holidays, and 20 days paid vacation, leisure time in Belgium amounts to nearly 150 days a year. Free time is used on various activities. There are striking differences between the social classes: people with a higher education and a higher income spend more time and money on leisure.

GETTING OUTDOORS

Belgians are great sun worshipers. Some people joke that when the sun comes out, the Belgians are rescued from mental breakdowns and even strangers start being friendly to each other! Because so much of the year is cold and rainy, people tend to head outdoors whenever possible.

Surprisingly perhaps, considering this love of the sun, many Belgians prefer to spend their vacations in their own country. Whereas their Dutch and German neighbors invade the beaches of southern Europe in great numbers, Belgians seem far more content to head for their own North Sea beaches or to go hiking in the Ardennes. Belgium's extensive canal system adds another dimension to vacations, and nothing could be more typically Belgian than hiring a pleasure boat and cruising along the inland waterways. Vacations are usually taken in summer, although more young people are choosing winter vacations.

Many amusement and theme parks cater to the growing recreational industry. These include waterparks, old steam trains, zoos, safari parks, and an indoor ski center that manufactures "real" snow.

Opposite: **Canoeing on the Semois river in southern Belgium is one of many summer pleasures.**

The Belgian coast attracts tourists in any season.

People relax and soak up the sun at a terrace café.

Belgians love to catch up with each other over a drink at the local café or pub, where time is also spent listening to popular music or playing games. Cards and board games are very popular, and some cafés even run a local chess club.

Art lovers enjoy an extensive selection of museums and art galleries throughout the country, and great art exhibitions are organized in the major cities. These are often sponsored by the Belgian railways, which issue special travel packages. Once a year, on the occasion of the Open Monuments Day, private and official buildings in Brussels open their doors to the public. For only one day, art and architecture lovers can view hidden treasures along an itinerary that takes the visitor all over the city. On other days, the culturally inclined can visit many cultural centers that open their galleries, libraries, and theaters to the public. The centers often include music and dance schools and organize activities.

Going outdoors also means attending a show or going to the movies, even in this era of television and satellites. In the suburbs around the major cities, massive movie theaters show the latest local and international films, and audiences are growing.

BELGIAN DOGS

Dog breeding is a famous activity in Belgium, and Belgian breeders have produced several species of dogs, many of which were specially bred to work on farms. Today some of these breeds work with the police force and are also popular abroad.

The Belgian sheepdog weighs between 55 and 60 pounds and is identified by its heavy tail and neck ruff. The Belgian Malinois is a short-haired version of the sheepdog and is often used in police work.

The Belgian Tervuren was first bred in the town of the same name. It differs from other sheepdogs because of its rich mahogany coat. The Tervuren is believed to make a particularly good companion.

HOBBIES

Belgians enjoy a whole range of hobbies. On a walk through any large town, you will see shops catering to the needs of stamp collectors, model makers, and toy-train collectors, as well as numerous pet shops. Many Belgians are keen antique collectors who like hunting in antique dealers' shops and at numerous markets held in every town. For those who cannot afford rare paintings or vases, collectable items of all sorts can be found.

Every town also has clubs and societies that might include sport clubs, cultural circles, choirs, amateur theater, brass bands, youth clubs, senior citizens' clubs, and political groups. The most popular hobby is probably gardening, which is often the major pastime for people living in the countryside.

The nation has a soft spot for pets, with cats, dogs, and caged birds being the favorites. Tanks with tropical fish and North Sea flora and fauna decorate many a living room. Caged birds of all sorts can be purchased in markets. Unfortunately, Belgium has perhaps been a little behind the rest of Europe in controlling the capture of wild birds and regulating the import of rare species.

Special pet markets, held on Sundays, make it hard for visitors to resist the charm of cuddly puppies and kittens.

Redu is a small village in the south of Belgium with 23 bookshops, 5 art galleries, and 10 little cafés. Some 10 workshops specialize in crafts such as paper-making, printing, and bookbinding. Once a year, the Book Weekend attracts hundreds of book amateurs and second-hand book dealers, who set up stalls along the streets.

READING

It is difficult to describe the Belgian public as a reading public. Belgium can be proud of well-known authors in both major linguistic regions, reading is encouraged in schools by the provision of well-stocked libraries, and major book fairs are held. Nonetheless, only 5 out of 10 Belgians have read an entire book! Most of the regular readers are young people and women.

The higher the educational level reached, the more people read, but it also seems that as people grow older they read less. Newspapers and weekly and monthly magazines are much more popular: about 7 out of 10 people read the papers almost every day.

TELEVISION

Belgians seem to watch less television than their European neighbors. It would be unusual to see a family watching television in the daytime or during meals. The arrival of satellite television and the opening of more regional stations may bring rapid changes to the nation's viewing habits.

There are two domestic broadcasting stations, one run by the government and the other private. Generally, the government station broadcasts more cultural and educational programs. Programs are bilingual and not interrupted by commercials. The private station has a more popular range of programs, such as family games and sitcoms.

Being a small nation with a limited audience means Belgian television cannot afford to make many programs of its own and so must buy shows from other countries. The French region naturally favors programs made in France, but both stations show programs from Britain and the United States. In Flemish regions, these will generally be shown in English with subtitles. In Wallonia, the programs are usually dubbed into French.

Radio is still very popular; people at home usually tune in to their
favorite station during the day. It is not at all unusual to have the radio
playing quietly in offices and factories. Cafés and bars might also play the
radio during the day. There are three main government stations: Radio 1
broadcasts documentaries and cultural programs; Radio 2 is the pop
station; and Radio 3 specializes in other types of music, such as classical
and jazz. On the other hand, a wide range of local "free radios" broadcast
in small towns and villages, usually offering nonstop popular music.

THE LOTTERY

Gambling is not deeply embedded in Belgian culture. The only forms of
gambling that have captured the public are the state-run lottery and lucky
draws, such as LOTTO and Joker. In the lottery, people buy books of
tickets; they win if their number is among those drawn.

In the LOTTO, people buy cards with a series of numbers on them.
Each week numbers are pulled out of a hat, and cardholders see how
many of those numbers appear on their cards. Usually in the LOTTO there
are several joint winners who divide the prize, but whenever there is a
single winner, the prize can come to millions of francs.

Paths along Belgium's canals are free of automobile traffic and are ideal tracks for amateur or professional cyclists.

CYCLING

Cycling is the national sport of Belgium, and every weekend thousands of people go riding in the countryside. For many people, cycling is an important way to make a social statement. Their bicycle must be of the best quality available, and their clothing are copies of the fashions worn by professional racers. Other people just keep an old "bone shaker" for making short trips around town. So many people use bicycles for local transport that it can sometimes be difficult to find a space in the bicycle parking zones.

Several touring circuits have been set up around the country. The most ambitious is the Vlaanderen route, which covers 398 miles (641 kilometers) on side tracks and special cycle paths. At the end of each day's ride, there are hostels and camping sites. Most of Belgium is flat, which makes cycling easy; this is probably the reason the sport has grown to be so popular.

For more serious riders, there is a strong network of clubs where members train together for competitions. At the top level, Belgium stages a whole series of world-class races, including the Tour of Belgium, which is considered one of the top events on the cycling calendar. However, nothing in professional cycling compares with the excitement of the Tour de France, which usually passes through Belgium at some stage to let Belgian racing fans enjoy the spectacle. Belgian cyclists have a good record in the event—one of the most famous Belgian cyclists of all time is Eddy Merckx, who won the Tour de France for four years in a row.

SOCCER

Soccer may be considered to be another national sport, together with cycling. Extremely popular with Belgian men, it is played at all levels and by all age groups. In the villages, the soccer team is often an important part of the local social life. Dances and other events, organized for the community, help to raise a little money to run the team.

At the professional level, Belgium has a strong league that plays games on Saturday evening or Sunday afternoon and is supported in the stadiums or on television by enthusiastic fans. FC Anderlecht is the most famous club and has won the Belgian championship more than 20 times. The professional clubs often field one or two players from overseas, including many from Africa and Eastern Europe. Some of Belgium's own star players will spend part of their careers in Germany, Spain, or Italy where they can earn far more money.

OTHER SPORTS

The jogging craze has caught on in Belgium, and each weekend sees a program of fun runs and races, with the Brussels Marathon being one of the major events for men and women.

Over the years, Belgium has also produced several excellent long- and middle-distance

Spring and summer are the ideal seasons for joggers.

Some Belgian stables are well known for their excellent horses, which are trained very seriously and run in races and equestrian shows. A lot of people simply enjoy riding along the coasts or in the forests.

runners. Back in the 1960s, Gaston Roelants was Olympic champion in the steeplechase, and nearly 10 years later, Emiel Puttemans was an Olympic silver medallist. At the 1976 Olympics in Montreal, Ivo Van Damme won two silver medals and looked likely to become a future world champion. He was tragically killed while driving back home from a track meeting. The Ivo Van Damme Memorial Meeting, staged in August, is now an important fixture on the European track and field circuit.

Besides jogging, people enjoy playing an amazingly wide range of sports. Basketball, volleyball, and table tennis are popular for both amateurs and professionals, and matches are largely attended and often covered on television. The Japanese martial arts are widely practiced by people of all ages.

People seldom think of the Belgians playing golf, but the country has over 52 clubs. The Royal Antwerp Club was founded in 1888, making it one of the oldest in the world. Golf was introduced by British workers who came to Belgium in the last century to help build railways and factories. Other sports, such as rugby and *pétanque* ("peh-TAHNK"—a bowling game), have made their way across the border from France and have a strong following in Wallonia.

Belgians also love a great spectacle with noise and color, so all types of motor sports are popular. Motocross has produced a string of Belgian world champions such as Joel Robert (late 1960s) and George Jobe (1980s). As they race around the course, the bikes go flying into the air and splashing through the mud, much to the delight of the spectators. The Belgian Grand Prix is one of the major races on the Formula One circuit and is an important day in the Belgian sports calendar. Two race tracks in Belgium are capable of staging the top races: Heusden-Zolder and the slightly better known Spa-Francorchamps.

PIGEON RACING

Belgium, along with the north of England, can claim to be the founder and home of pigeon racing. Many special species of racing pigeons have been bred around Antwerp, and Belgium founded the international body that governs the sport.

Pigeon racing is particularly strong in the rural regions and is very much a male activity. It is also seen as an activity for older people, although many men teach the sport to their sons. The *duivenmelker* ("DEUY-vuhn-mehl-kuhr"), or pigeon racer, plans the breeding program in the hope of producing champions, trains them for the big events, and bets on them as well.

Races are governed by strict rules. The pigeons are handed over to the race officials in the hometown and taken away in a van to be released together. Races generally start over short distances and get longer as the season progresses. By the end of a racing year, the birds might be taken as far as southern France before being released to find their way back. They usually fly at 40 miles per hour (64 kilometers per hour), but if there is a strong wind behind them, they can go much faster. When the pigeons are due to arrive home, the nervous owner tries to keep everybody in the house quiet, as pigeons might not land if there is any noise. As soon as a pigeon lands, the ring is removed from its foot and placed into a special time clock that records the finishing time for the bird. The sealed clock is taken to the club headquarters, where the pigeon racer discovers how his champion bird has performed against its rivals. Half the fun of pigeon racing is the social side, and most owners spend the afternoons in discussion with fellow racers.

FESTIVALS

THERE ARE 10 national holidays a year in Belgium. In addition, Belgium has carnivals and processions, some of them very colorful occasions when hundreds of people dress up in amazing costumes.

CHRISTMAS

Christmas is a main holiday in Belgium. School closes for a two-week holiday, and although factories and offices do not enjoy such a long break, work does slow down.

The first important date in the Christmas season is November 11. Although it is Armistice Day, in certain parts of the country it is also a day when St. Maarten, or Santa Claus, brings presents to children. According to tradition, Santa arrives in Belgium on December 6; on the evening before, children leave out a large shoe or boot for him to fill with presents.

Belgian children visit Santa Claus and hope he has brought the presents they wished for during the night.

Opposite: **For a few days each summer, the Brussels Grand Place is decorated with a floral carpet, showing designs related to the city's history.**

In Belgium, Santa is traditionally portrayed as riding a horse. Black Peter, usually a white man with a blackened face, rides beside Santa on a donkey. It is actually Black Peter who has the job of climbing down the chimney to leave presents, as well as oranges and sweets.

After rushing downstairs in the morning to find their presents, children still have to go to school, but as can be imagined, little work gets done. In the elementary school, it is quite likely that somebody will dress up as

Santa Claus, and the children can enjoy a second visit from him. But life at this time is not all fun, for soon after this, children face important school exams.

As Christmas approaches, people decorate their house, and possibly the trees in the garden, with lights and ornaments. This is also the time to send cards to family and friends. The Belgian post office offers special rates for Christmas cards and issues attractive stamps. A white Christmas is quite unusual; snow usually does not fall until January.

The Christmas Eve meal is an important family occasion, and rabbit is the traditional dish. Many families, even those who do not usually go to church, attend the Midnight Mass. Christmas Day is often a time to visit relatives, and lunch is the main meal of the day. On Christmas Day, everybody exchanges presents, not just the children.

At Christmas time, most towns and cities set up impressive decorations in the main square.

NEW YEAR

New Year's Eve has far less tradition attached to it and generally is simply a time to go out and enjoy oneself. This might mean going to a party or arranging a meal at a restaurant. Toward midnight, people might gather in the town center to see the year in together.

NATIONAL AND COMMUNITY HOLIDAYS

Belgium's National Day is celebrated on July 21, the anniversary of the day King Leopold I first took his oath. There are celebrations throughout the country, with some of the biggest events taking place in Brussels. Processions and free entertainment are organized in many of the parks, and the celebration usually ends with fireworks.

A Belgian in the costume of a soldier during the celebration of the Battle of the Golden Spurs.

Communities also celebrate their own special days. The Flemish community celebrates the anniversary of the Battle of the Golden Spurs on July 11. The French community selected September 27, the day patriots in Brussels enjoyed a victory over the Dutch. The German-speaking community celebrates its national day on November 15.

Armistice Day, November 11, is the day World War I came to an end, and it is a national holiday for everyone. The holiday means more to older people who remember the world wars. Special services take place at the sites of battlefields, and flowers are placed at war monuments. Churches hold special services for people who gave their lives for their country, and old soldiers proudly put on their uniforms again.

107

BINCHE: CARNIVAL TOWN

The little town of Binche in southern Belgium is considered the traditional home of carnivals as it stages a yearly celebration that can be traced back to the 14th century. The key figures are the *Gilles* ("JEEH-luh"), people wearing bright, colorful medieval costumes decorated with heraldic lions. Bells hang from their belts, and ostrich feathers are worn in their high hats. The *Gilles* dance all day and all night to the sound of brass bands and drums, and they go around town throwing oranges to the crowd. The festival ends with a procession and the lighting of a giant bonfire.

Nobody is quite sure how this carnival started, but it was probably brought by the Spanish occupiers and celebrates the victory of Emperor Charles V over the Incas of South America. Binche is also home to the international Carnival and Costume Museum, where carnival costumes and masks from around the world are displayed in the old Augustine College.

CARNIVALS AND OTHER EVENTS

Some special events fall neatly into categories: pre-Lent carnivals, May Day celebrations, harvest celebrations, beer festivals, and historic parades. Other celebrations, including some carnivals, are difficult to categorize.

Carnivals are deeply ingrained in the Belgian culture, and most people join in the fun. The committees that organize them often work all year to prepare for the big day. To make the event a success, they rely on the help of clubs, schools, and bands in the town.

Soon after the New Year, the first of the carnivals begins, with the town of Ronse starting the program in January. After that, hardly a week passes until Easter that a carnival isn't taking place somewhere. Malmédy's celebration lasts four days, with bands, plays, and a giant *conga* dance that snakes its way through the streets, before ending with a bonfire. The carnival in the Flemish town of Aalst also has a unique feel to it. It begins on a Sunday in February with the day of the giants, Monday sees "the throwing of the onions," and the celebration ends with the "dirty aunts" parading through the street in costume.

Small towns and villages have their own Easter parade, such as this one in Hakendover.

EASTER CELEBRATION AND PROCESSIONS

In many ways, Easter in Belgium is almost identical to the celebration in the United States. Cards are sent to friends and chocolate eggs given as gifts. One event that does have a special Belgian feel to it takes place at Beloeil Castle near Mons in southern Belgium. Here children hunt for Easter eggs on the castle grounds. The Easter holiday also sees some of the largest congregations of the year gather in churches around the country.

Among the Easter parades is the Procession of Penitents, where cloaked and hooded participants carry heavy wooden crosses through the streets. The most famous parade is the Procession of the Holy Blood, which takes place in Brugge on Ascension Day. Hundreds of people dress up as figures from the Bible and march through the streets. At the center of the procession are the priests carrying a receptacle said to contain drops of blood from Jesus.

Mons has its own Procession of the Golden Carriage. This celebration ends with a fight between St. George and the dragon to show the struggle between good and evil.

During the *Ommegang*, the center of Brussels is closed to traffic to allow the parade to pass through the streets.

HISTORICAL PARADES

Some of Belgium's parades and festivals are a reconstruction of historic events. The most famous celebration in Brussels is the *Ommegang* ("OHM-muh-gang") in July, which is modeled on a parade staged before Charles V in 1549. In the evening, more than 2,000 of the city's residents dress up in medieval costume and parade into the Grand Place. The parade includes horse riders, stilt walkers, jesters, soldiers, aristocrats, and finally the imperial family and their court. Even *Manneken-Pis* joins in the celebration and is dressed in a special festival costume.

Brugge has a medieval parade called the Procession of the Golden Tree that takes place only every five years. It stages the 1468 wedding between Charles the Bold and Princess Margaret of York.

Ieper is famous for the Festival of Cats, which dates back to the Middle Ages and the belief that cats were linked to the devil. To disprove this idea, Count Baudouin had all the cats taken to the tower of the town hall and thrown off to show they were mortal. This bloody and bizarre spectacle went on until the last century. Today only soft toys are thrown from the tower. The festival also has a magnificent parade with bands, medieval costumes, and, of course, giant cats.

In August, giant figures, some 13 feet (4 meters) tall, parade through the town of Ath. The French character of the town is reflected in the parade; the giants often look like Napoleon's soldiers with costumes of red, white, and blue. The highlight of the parade is a fight between David and Goliath.

FESTIVALS FOR THE SEASONS

Once Easter is over, towns start preparing for their May Day celebrations. These involve street parades, often with a May Queen, and Maypole dancing. Flower festivals also take place, and town squares and halls around the country are laid out with a carpet of flowers, bringing magnificent color to the grand old squares and celebrating the summer season. The largest and most famous flower carpet is laid out in Gent each September. It displays an amazing variety of local and exotic flowers and offers a last chance to enjoy the flower season before winter starts. As winter approaches, the traditional harvest festivals are celebrated.

May to September is the season of the *Marches*. People dress up in old military uniforms, usually from the age of Napoleon, and march from town to town. There are bands, drums, pipes, and gunfire. A few people might dress as officers and ride alongside, adding more color to the event. The *Marches* take place only in Wallonia, and mainly south of Charleroi, in the province of Hainaut.

The *Marches* probably date back to the 16th century, although some believe the tradition goes even farther back. The most likely explanation is that, at the time, the roads were dangerous places and military escorts had to be provided when religious relics were transported from town to town. Today the *Marches* are still dedicated to saints. Whatever the reason behind them, the *Marches* are a wonderful social event and add another dimension to the country's pageantry.

The biggest *Marches* can involve up to 5,000 people, as well as all their supporters and families. The Gerpinnes march is the longest and covers 22 miles (35 kilometers).

FOOD

THROUGHOUT ITS TURBULENT history of foreign occupation, Belgian cuisine has absorbed culinary influences from both Latin and Germanic cultures. Belgians will tell you that food in their country is better than anywhere else, and anyone traveling around the country will notice that the Belgians take eating very seriously.

Belgium has built up a long tradition of cooking. Flemish Benedictine monks improved beer brewing techniques, and another Fleming, Charles de l'Escluse, played an important role in publicizing the potato throughout Europe. Belgians are proud of some unique specialities that are often referred to in old cookbooks.

Belgian cuisine offers its gastronomic variety in local dishes made out of ancient recipes and using readily available ingredients. The most obvious regional contributions have been game animals, such as venison, partridge, and hare from the Ardennes, and seafood from the North Sea.

Many Belgian towns also have developed their own specialities. Liège is home to the *salade Liègeoise* ("sah-LAH-duh lee-a-JWAH-zuh"), which combines bacon, potatoes, onions, parsley, and French beans to create a unique dish. The Liège region is also famous for stews and soups. Gent has contributed the famous *Waterzooi* ("WAH-tuhr-zoohj") soup, once made from fish, but now just as likely to be cooked from chicken. Brussels has pioneered the art of cooking with beer, as well as giving the nation the world-famous Belgian waffles.

Cooking in Belgium is strongly influenced by the availability of different foods with the changing seasons. People eagerly wait for the *primeurs* ("pree-MEUH-rs"), or early vegetables and fruits of the season, while restaurants organize special gastronomic events. Herrings are best in spring, May and June bring fresh asparagus and juicy strawberries, and fall is the start of the hunting season and the arrival of wild game in the shops.

Raw ingredients for the night's cooking are often displayed on a cart or table in front of a restaurant. A seafood display is first packed with ice, then lobsters, prawns, and crabs are carefully placed within a border of fresh vegetables. An enormous fish, its mouth gaping, forms a dramatic centerpiece. Artistically decorated boards advertise the speciality of the day.

Opposite: **Belgians tend to eat out in restaurants a great deal, and Brussels has more restaurants than London, although the British capital is eight times bigger.**

Markets are popular places where people stop for a friendly chat while they shop.

MARKETS VERSUS SUPERMARKETS

The pattern of shopping in Belgium has changed drastically over the last 30 years. Small groceries, specialty shops, and markets used to be the only places that sold food and other supplies, but the big supermarkets are taking more and more of the trade. Still, markets remain important: a place to find fresh food, flowers, and bargains and to have an enjoyable day out. Markets are often held on Sundays, when the big malls are closed. In cities with a high concentration of immigrants, markets tend to be a colorful international happening. The Brussels Midi Market offers exotic delicacies from Italian pepper cheese and Turkish olives to African salted fish. Small shops in town and in the villages offer convenience and special service. Local bakeries stock a daily range of fresh breads, rolls, pastries, and cakes. The local butcher offers all sorts of cold and cooked meats. The main street delicatessens tempt customers with displays of cold meats, fish, salads, and cheeses.

114

MEAT

Meat forms an important part of Belgian cuisine, and steak with chips is probably the nation's favorite meal. Pork and chicken are also eaten regularly, and rabbit is far more popular in Belgium than in any other European country. Indeed, there is a whole range of recipes created just for rabbit: cooked in a casserole with beer or cooked with prunes are the most popular ways. Many Belgian recipes make use of kidneys, liver, and other offal. Pigs' ears and feet are used in favorite hot-pot dishes.

Belgians can choose from an amazing range of sausages, many being seasoned with herbs and spices. Ham and paté from the Ardennes and salami are also popular.

Some of the dishes are more typically prepared during winter and tend to be hearty and hot. Favorite meat dishes include *Vlaamse karbonade* ("VLAAHM-suh khar-boh-NAH-duh"), a tasty beef stew cooked in a special local beer; *Faisan à la Brabançonne* ("fuh-SAHN ah lah brah-bahn-SOH-nuh"), pheasant braised with endive; jugged hare in beer with onions and prunes; *Waterzooi*, fish or chicken cooked in a soup with potatoes, carrots, leeks, and cream; *Konijn met pruimen* ("koh-NEYHN meht PREU-muhn"), rabbit with prunes; and pheasant served with braised Belgian endive.

Ham, paté, sausages, and other cooked meat products can be found in specialty shops.

SEAFOOD

Seafood is very popular in Belgium, and few sights are more typical than a group of diners in a seaside restaurant enjoying a steaming pot of mussels. Herbs are particularly important when cooking mussels, with onions, celery, and parsley giving that special Belgian flavor.

Belgium's North Sea shrimps are said to be the best in the world. A few fishers, in bright yellow oilskins, still catch these the traditional way, which involves using the strong Brabant horses to trawl a net through waist-high water. The shrimps are boiled in salted water and may be eaten plain, together with a cool Belgian beer. The most typical way to serve them is to fill a tomato with a mixture of shrimp and mayonnaise.

Inland, river fish form another Belgian delicacy, with *paling in het groen* ("PAH-ling ihn hut GROON"), eel cooked in a parsley sauce and served cold, and *truite au bleu* ("trweet oh bleuh"), trout cooked with carrots, leeks, and potatoes, being the favorites.

116

CHEESY BELGIAN ENDIVE AND HAM

serves 4

8 heads of endive	grated cheese
8 slices cooked ham	seasoning: salt, pepper, grated nutmeg
$1/4$ pint milk	1 tablespoon cornstarch
1 tablespoon butter	breadcrumbs

Boil the heads of endive in salted water for about 20 minutes, or until they are tender. Drain the liquid and set it aside. Roll a slice of ham around each piece of endive, and lay them flat in a buttered dish.

Boil milk with one cup of the liquid set aside, and stir in a tablespoon of butter and four tablespoons of grated cheese. Season with salt, pepper, and grated nutmeg. Thicken sauce with 1 tablespoon cornstarch and pour over the rolled ham and endive. Sprinkle with breadcrumbs and grated cheese and brown in the oven under the broiler.

SPECIAL VEGETABLES

Few cities in the world have a vegetable named after them, but Brussels sprouts are world-famous. The first record of Brussels sprouts being eaten in Belgium dates to 1587, but they were probably part of the diet three or four centuries before. Sprouts grow best in cool climates and are damaged in hot weather. An excellent source of vitamins A and C, sprouts are enjoyed most in winter.

Witloof, or chicory (Belgian endive), appears with typical hearty winter dishes.

Particularly prized is the Belgian asparagus, eaten in Belgium since Roman times. People favor the thick, white spears and their rich flavor. The best asparagus comes from the sandy soils of the region around Mechelen.

Witloof ("WHIT-loohf"), or chicory (Belgian endive), has not become so universally popular, but it is often eaten in Belgium and the surrounding areas of France, Germany, and the Netherlands. Belgians use both the leaves as a salad and the roots as a vegetable. As a vegetable, endive is usually boiled and served with butter, although it is used in different ways in different recipes. Other popular vegetables include red cabbage and leeks.

The typical Belgian chip, eaten as a snack, is long and thick. A thinner variety, called *lucifers*, is served with fine Belgian dishes.

BELGIAN CHIPS

Belgians and Britons both claim to be the inventor of the fried potato, and so do the Spanish and even some French. Known in Belgium as the *friet* ("FREEHT") in Flemish or *frite* ("FREEH-tuh") in French and in England as the chip, the fried potato made its way to the rest of the world as the French fry.

Fried potatoes are a favorite Belgian street food, and Belgians tend to eat them the same way as Americans eat popcorn. Although the *frites* or *frieten* often are served at meals, they are usually served from mobile canteens or small huts. They are handed over to customers in paper cones or on small cardboard trays and topped off with a large portion of mayonnaise and salt. Belgian *frites* have a special flavor because they are fried twice in hot oil, to cook the inside first and then to brown the outside.

THE MEAL PATTERN

Even if the family has to get to work, breakfast still tends to be a surprisingly relaxed occasion. People usually sit down together and take half an hour over the meal. Breakfast is generally light: rolls or bread with jam or an egg, and tea, coffee, milk, or hot chocolate. On weekends, sweet delicacies are served: *craquelin* ("krah-kuh-LAIN"), soft sweet bread; *cramique* ("krah-ME-kuh") or *kramiek* ("krah-MEEK"), sweet bread with currants; and butter or chocolate rolls.

Lunch is often brought from home, with sandwiches naturally being very popular because they are convenient. Schools and large companies or factories outside the cities provide hot meals at a small cost. These usually include a soup, a main course with meat, vegetables, and potatoes, and a small dessert.

Dinner might consist of a light meal, such as sandwiches or salads, but usually people have an evening meal that is similar to lunch. In recent years, health trends have begun to alter the nation's eating habits. Belgian chefs who once boasted that cooking was all about taste, butter, and flour are having to make some concessions toward high fiber, low-fat diets.

Sunday lunch is the most important meal of the week. It is a time for the family and relatives to sit together in a relaxed atmosphere. Several dishes, desserts, wines, and beers may be served during the afternoon.

There is little that is different about a Belgian kitchen from a typical kitchen in the United States. However, a few items in the cutlery collection might surprise visitors, like the tiny forks for prizing snails out of their shells.

Belgium is home to hundreds of regional cheeses, some of which are produced in the old monasteries that still use traditional methods. Many of these, such as Passendale, Rubens, Wynendale, and Maredsous, are virtually unheard of outside of Belgium.

119

DESSERTS

A nation that likes food so much is naturally going to be expert when it comes to dessert. Some desserts are traditionally associated with towns or regions, for example, *kletskoppen* ("KLEH-ts-koh-puhn," crunchy sweet cookies) originally came from Brugge, and *tarte aldjote* ("TAHRT ahl-DJOH-tuh," beet leaves and cheese) from Nivelles. Gent has special little cakes called *Gentse mokken* ("GHENT-suh MOHK-kun"), and Brussels contributes its famous waffles, served with sugar, butter, fresh cream, and fresh fruit.

Nationwide favorites include white cheesecake, *speculoos* ("SPEH-kuh-loohs," crunchy gingerbread with coffee), and chocolate mouse. *Dame blanche* ("DHAM BLAHNSJ") is another favorite made of vanilla ice cream with hot chocolate sauce. Juicy red strawberries have a special place in Belgian desserts and can be served with cream or used to decorate other desserts. Strawberries are now available through much of the year because special farms grow them in greenhouses, but the high strawberry season still happens to be during the summer months of June and July.

Belgian chocolate is world famous and includes the typical *pralines* ("prah-LEEHN"), which are sold in special stores, where they are displayed like precious items in a jewelry shop. The choice of fillings is endless and includes coffee, chocolate cream, marzipan, liqueur, and even whole cherries with the stem still attached. Most of the best pralines use fresh cream and so do not keep long, although that is seldom a problem!

Belgian *pralines:* any shop assistant will happily make up an assorted collection to meet the taste of each customer.

A BEER TO EVERYONE'S TASTE

Beer is the great national drink, and Belgium produces around 400 types of beer. Some of them are brewed in small local breweries and are not available outside the immediate region. The whole range includes blond, dark, and white beers, the last using up to 45% wheat.

Serving a good beer is an art mastered only after some practice.

For centuries, monasteries have been a great source of brews, and in the past the revenue this produced was particularly important to them. A handful of monasteries still produce beer using old recipes developed by monks, the most famous of which is the Chimay Monastery for its dark, strong *Trappiste* ("trah-PEE-st") beer.

The area southwest of Brussels, called *Pajottenland* ("pah-JOHT-tuhn-land"), is famous for its *Lambik* ("lahm-BEEHK") and *Gueuze* ("GHEU-zuh") beers, still made by the traditional methods. The brews use wheat and barley and are left for one night in open wooden tubs while natural fermentation starts. At this stage, a few wild hops that grow in the region are added. The brews are then left to mature in the barrels for up to two years. The result is a golden-colored beer that tastes a little like apple juice. Fruit, such as cherries or raspberries, is sometimes added while the beer is maturing to produce a beer with a surprising taste.

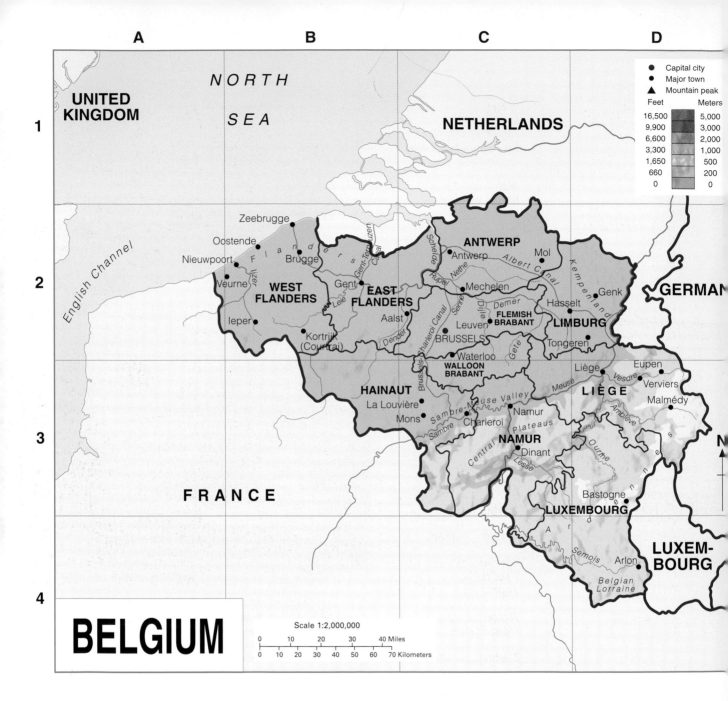

NORTH

SEA

UNITED
KINGDOM

NETHERLANDS

1

Feet	Meters
●	Capital city
●	Major town
▲	Mountain peak

Feet	Meters
16,500	5,000
9,900	3,000
6,600	2,000
3,300	1,000
1,650	500
660	200
0	0

English Channel

Zeebrugge

Oostende

Nieuwpoort

Brugge

Flanders

ANTWERP

Antwerp

Mol

Albert Canal

Kempenland

GERMAN

2

Veurne

WEST
FLANDERS

Gent

EAST
FLANDERS

Schelde

Rupel

Nethe

Mechelen

Dijle

Demer

FLEMISH
BRABANT

Hasselt

LIMBURG

Genk

Ieper

Aalst

Leie

Dender

Brussels-Charleroi Canal

Senne

Leuven

BRUSSELS

Gete

Tongeren

Kortrijk
(Courtrai)

Waterloo

WALLOON
BRABANT

Liège

LIÈGE

Eupen

Verviers

Vesdre

Malmédy

Meuse

HAINAUT

La Louvière

Mons

Sambre

Meuse Valley

Namur

NAMUR

Central Plateaus

Dinant

Lesse

Ambléve

Ourthe

3

Sambre

Charleroi

Bastogne

LUXEMBOURG

LUXEM-
BOURG

FRANCE

Semois

Arlon

Belgian
Lorraine

4

BELGIUM

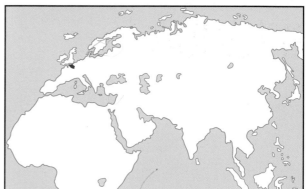

QUICK NOTES

OFFICIAL NAME
Kingdom of Belgium

LAND AREA
11,781 square miles (30,513 square kilometers)

POPULATION
9,958,000 (1994)

CAPITAL
Brussels

MAIN CITIES
Antwerp, Gent, Charleroi, Liège

PROVINCES
French speaking: Walloon Brabant, Hainaut, Liège, Luxembourg, Namur
Flemish speaking: Flemish Brabant, East Flanders, West Flanders, Antwerp, Limburg

MAJOR RIVERS
Schelde, Meuse

NATIONAL LANGUAGES
Flemish, French, and German are the three national languages. Flemish, a version of Dutch, is spoken in the north, French is spoken in the south, and German is spoken by a small minority in the east of the country. English is learned in school and widely spoken as a third language.

NATIONAL ANTHEM
The Brabant Song

NATIONAL FLAG
Three broad vertical stripes. The colors are, from left to right, black, yellow, and red.

HIGHEST POINT
Mt. Botrange (2,277 feet / 694 meters)

RELIGIONS
Roman Catholicism
Islam and Protestantism have a small number of followers.

CURRENCY
Belgian franc
US$1 = 35 Belgian francs

MEASUREMENTS
Metric system

MAIN PRODUCTS
Chemicals, agricultural products, cement, glass, textiles, paper, steel.

KINGS SINCE INDEPENDENCE
Leopold I (1831–1865)
Leopold II (1865–1909)
Albert I (1909–1934)
Leopold III (1934–1950)
Baudouin I (1950–1993)
Albert II (ascended throne in 1993)

LIFE EXPECTANCY
Women: 79
Men: 72

GLOSSARY

Begijnhof ("buh-GEYEN-hohf")
Religious homes where women could enjoy company and security in a religious atmosphere.

craquelin ("krah-kuh-LAIN")
A soft, sweet bread.

cramique (French, "krah-ME-kuh")
kramiek (Flemish, "krah-MEEK")
A sweet bread with currants.

duivenmelker ("DEUY-vuhn-mehl-khur")
Person who breeds pigeons to race, a favorite Belgian sport.

friet (Flemish, "FREEHT")
frite (French, "FREEH-tuh")
Belgian-style French fries.

Gilles ("JEEH-luh")
Participants in the Binche carnival, who wear a brightly colored medieval costume. They go around town throwing oranges to the public.

La Belgitude ("LAH behl-ji-TUU-duh")
Belgian art movement at the beginning of the 20th century that developed a national feeling.

Les Marolles ("LEH mah-ROHL")
Old working-class area in the center of Brussels where a dialect is spoken.

Marollien ("mah-roh-LYEAN")
Typical dialect of the Marolles, a version of French mixed with Flemish words and even some Spanish. The dialect is now disappearing.

Ommegang ("OHM-muh-gang")
Historical parade held in Brussels, a reenactment of a parade held for Charles V in 1549.

pétanque ("peh-TAHNK")
Game of bowls where the ball is tossed into the air instead of along the ground.

polders ("POHL-duhrs")
Area in the Lowlands, or Flanders, region consisting of thin, sandy soil, with clay underneath.

pralines ("prah-LEEHN")
Belgian chocolates.

primeurs ("pree-MEUH-rs")
Vegetables and fruits eaten at the very beginning of their season.

speculoos ("SPEH-kuh-loohs")
Crunchy gingerbread.

taalvrijheid ("TAAHL-vreye-heyet")
The right to use Flemish as an official language, claimed by the Flemings.

Tarte aldjote ("TARHT ahl-DJOH-tuh")
Typical Walloon cake made of beet leaves and cheese.

Wallon ("wah-LOHN")
Group of French dialects spoken in Wallonia, with origins in the old Celtic and Germanic languages.

Waterzooi ("WAH-tuhr-zoohj")
Typical Flemish dish, made of fish or chicken cooked in a soup with potatoes, carrots, leeks, and cream.

witloof ("WHIT-loohf")
Belgian endive, also called chicory, a popular white vegetable used in salad or cooked.

BIBLIOGRAPHY

Lerner Publications. *Belgium in Pictures*. Minneapolis, MN: Lerner Publications Co., 1991.

Riley, Raymond Charles. *Belgium*. Santa Barbara, California: ABC-CLIO, Inc., 1989.

Wickman, Stephen B. *Belgium, A Country Study*. Washington, D.C.: U.S. Government Printing Office, 1985.

INDEX

INDEX

INDEX